Critical Guides to French Texts

126 Balzac: Le Père Goriot

Critical Guides to French Texts

EDITED BY ROGER LITTLE, WOLFGANG VAN EMDEN, DAVID WILLIAMS

BALZAC

Le Père Goriot

Richard Bolster

Senior Lecturer in French
University of Bristol

Grant & Cutler
2000

© Grant & Cutler Ltd 2000
ISBN 0 7293 0426 4

DEPÓSITO LEGAL: V. 4.289 - 2000

Printed in Spain by
Artes Gráficas Soler, S.A., Valencia
for
GRANT & CUTLER LTD
55-57 GREAT MARLBOROUGH STREET, LONDON W1V 2AY

Contents

Contents

Prefatory Note

All quotations from *Le Père Goriot* relate to the following edition: Balzac, *Le Père Goriot*, introduction, notes, anthologie critique, bibliographie par Philippe Berthier, Paris, GF-Flammarion, 1995.

The source of other quotations and references may be found in the Select Bibliography at the end of this volume. Thus, '(3, p.12)' refers to page 12 in the third item in the Bibliography, namely *Lettres à Madame Hanska*.

1. Sources

'Vous serez bien fière du *Père Goriot*; mes amis prétendent que ce n'est comparable à rien, que c'est au-dessus de mes précédentes productions' (Balzac to Mme Hanska, *3*, p. 279)

The novel *Le Père Goriot* aroused not only admiration but controversy at the time of its publication in 1834-35, and Balzac's best known work has continued to inspire a remarkable amount of comment and debate. In this short study it is not possible to give a detailed account of all the interesting contributions made by a variety of moralists, aesthetes, novelists, Marxists, Freudians and others, but to these predecessors I pay brief homage in my bibliography. To their opinions must be added that of Balzac, although we should study his comments without assuming that his self-knowledge was complete. He claimed that his intention was to be morally reassuring and politically conservative, but if he had really done this it is unlikely that he would have had so many readers over so many generations. In spite of his ambition to achieve historical accuracy, the Goriot story is inevitably a personal interpretation of the state of French society in the year 1819, a creation of the imagination more than a work of scientific observation. It portrays a specific Parisian setting which has disappeared, and an era which can at first appear distant from us, but his essential themes are not limited by space or time. He aspired to be a historian, but was firstly a novelist. It is true that *Le Père Goriot* can itself be considered as a historical document, even if one rejects the view that it is a serious historical study. In any case it is as a writer of fiction that Balzac lives on, and one cannot otherwise explain the continuing appeal of the story of Goriot and his daughters. Every educated French person knows what moral and social themes are represented by Rastignac and Vautrin.

When Balzac began writing the Goriot story in the late summer of 1834 he did not know that it would be a full-length novel, and one which would come to be seen as his finest work. His initial idea had been to produce a much shorter story on the single theme of the misfortunes of a Parisian father, and to do so with all possible speed because he was under contract to write a work of this sort for a periodical. It was a situation of pressure which he knew only too well, and not conducive to good writing. As he proceeded, the novelist progressively uncovered new aspects of the subject, and the work soon went far beyond the initial plan. The Goriot story was in fact a new and more extensive treatment of certain themes which had featured several times in his previous works. It also included a major structural innovation, the reintroduction of characters from earlier novels, which would for ever be linked with his name. The significance of this recurrence of characters, which would later be imitated by some major novelists, was that it gave readers who were familiar with Balzac's works an enhanced feeling that they were observing social reality with its web of relationships and repeated contacts. Each individual novel could be read on its own, but the whole seemed to have an extra dimension.

The account of the decline and death of Goriot was therefore presented as one thread woven into a pattern, as a single scene in the larger spectacle of contemporary life. Balzac later decided to call this greater drama *La Comédie humaine*, and it is significant that by doing so he chose to adopt the terminology of theatrical literature. His title also alludes to Dante's great poem, a fact which naturally drew much ridicule from his enemies, and which certainly did not reveal much modesty. His preface for the second edition of the Goriot story discusses the recurrence of his characters and comments amusingly on the fact that Mme de Restaud and Mme de Beauséant had already featured in *Gobseck* and in *La Femme abandonnée*, claiming that he had introduced these characters again in response to comments by some female readers. These ladies had complained to the novelist that his works contained an excessive number of unfaithful wives, and that he had portrayed them so favourably that some readers might be tempted to imitate them. This, said Balzac, had given him the idea of reintroducing the two characters in question so that he could not be accused of adding unnecessarily to the list of his adulterous heroines. This ironical account of the decision to use recurring characters for defensive reasons cannot be taken as a full explanation of his innovation, which has evident literary advantages, but it may contain part of the truth. It is certain that the amusing explanation given in the preface shows his awareness of the fact that much of his reputation can be attributed to the enthusiasm of female readers, which was in reality the case for all successful novelists, and demonstrates his eagerness to be attentive to their comments.

The interest of Balzac's female characters can be measured by comparing *Le Père Goriot* with any novel by Scott. Balzac sincerely admired the achievement of his famous predecessor, whose works had won him a reputation which was unprecedented for a novelist. He believed that the author of *Waverley* (1814) had changed the genre for ever, making it into a higher form of literature by combining fiction and history in a new manner. He saw that Scott had broken new ground by his use of physical descriptions of scenes and persons, and also by the manner in which he used direct speech. By the time he was writing the Goriot story, Balzac was so confident in his own ability that he saw himself not as an imitator of Scott but as a novelist who had learned from his admired colleague and who would further extend the frontier of the genre. Published in 1828, his work *Le Dernier Chouan ou la Bretagne en 1800* had been a piece of historical fiction in the manner of Scott. After this successful experiment he had set himself a new challenge, which was the adaptation of historical method to the portrayal of a very recent era, even to a period in which most of his readers had lived, and which in reality could be called contemporary.

Was it possible to comprehend and represent accurately the social reality of a period situated a mere decade and a half before the writing of a novel? Balzac felt that he could indeed adopt Scott's method and apply it to an era which was not distant in time, and also improve it by the introduction of certain new themes which were needed for the fuller portrayal of modern French society. Believing in addition that the limitation of Scott's novels was essentially their female characters, the author of *Le Père Goriot* intended to exploit the subject of relations between the sexes in a manner which would have been impossible in an increasingly puritanical Britain, even if

the circumspect author of *Waverley* had been personally capable of
it.

Balzac composed *Le Père Goriot* in a remarkable four months
when he was in his mid-thirties, fully confident in his abilities, and at
the peak of his creative powers. He later claimed that there had been
a specific source for the Goriot story, and that it was an account of
the actual misfortunes of a person known to him. This statement was
made in 1839 in the preface to his novel *Le Cabinet des antiques*
where it forms part of a discussion about the relationship between
fiction and reality. Balzac here asserted that he had felt obliged to
tone down the real facts of the case because they might have seemed
too strong in a work of fiction:

> L'auteur a déjà souvent répondu qu'il est souvent obligé
> d'atténuer la crudité de la nature. Quelques lecteurs ont
> traité *Le Père Goriot* comme une calomnie envers les
> enfants; mais l'événement qui a servi de modèle offrait
> des circonstances affreuses, et comme il ne s'en présente
> pas chez les Cannibales; le pauvre père a crié pendant
> vingt heures d'agonie pour avoir à boire, sans que
> personne arrivât à son secours, et ses deux filles étaient,
> l'une au bal, l'autre au spectacle, quoiqu'elles
> n'ignorassent pas l'état de leur père. Ce vrai-là n'eût pas
> été croyable. (*1*, vol. IV, p.962)

This explanation forms part of a discourse on the necessary
difference between art and life, and shows the sophistication of
Balzac's conception of the novel. His alleged real model for Goriot
may never have existed, but the fact that he made the claim is worthy
of note. So too is his assertion that a novelist has the right to alter
reality in order to give it a literary form which is culturally familiar
and acceptable. Art is necessarily a synthesis, he believed, and a
serious writer must therefore transform his material, since reality can
be too dramatic and too crude for literature.

Despite Balzac's assertion that he had taken the Goriot story
from real life it is possible that his essential inspiration was literary.
It is evident that fictional representations of filial ingratitude already
existed, since the various themes of family relationships are as old as

Oedipus. On April 10 1835, however, a malevolent article in the newspaper *Le Voleur* accused him of stealing the story from *Les Deux Gendres*, a popular comedy by Etienne. This attack was typical of the attitude of some journalists to a writer who was too successful and whose originality needed to be denied, but the evidence about the sources of the Goriot story leads towards a more prestigious literary model than the play by Etienne. This is Shakespeare's tragedy *King Lear*, which itself had been inspired by earlier literary sources. In this legendary tale Lear is a King of Britain who unwisely abdicates and shares his kingdom between two daughters who profess to love him greatly. Once they have power, the greedy and selfish nature of his daughters shows itself. The old man then experiences neglect and distress, before finally becoming mad, with a late moment of lucidity which completes the tragedy as he recognises his contribution to his downfall. Here are the essential elements of the Goriot story, in a vague and distant historical setting, and with characters from a different social class. Balzac adopts more than one element from the plot of *Lear*, for example the themes of rivalry between sisters, the conflicting interests of legitimate children and bastards, and even the subject of sexual antipathy between wife and husband. The situation of a good daughter unjustly rejected by her father is also in the Lear tragedy, as it is in *Le Père Goriot*. In addition, Rastignac's role as the friend and helper of Goriot resembles that of a character in Shakespeare's play, where Kent does his best to assist the fallen monarch.

This remarkable thematic similarity between the Lear story and that of Goriot does not indicate any lack of creative ability in Balzac. Subjects such as family tension, conflict between generations and sibling rivalry are the natural raw material of literature which is reworked by every generation of writers. *Le Père Goriot* contains not only a social transformation of the old theme, with a King of Britain being replaced by a modest Parisian merchant, it is also an extension of the subject. Exploiting the flexibility of the novel genre in which there are no constraints of space and time, Balzac provides a crowd of characters who could not be accommodated in a play. Another change made possible by the adaptation of the Lear story to the novel genre was the provision of a more subtle psychological portrayal, and his portrait of the selfish daughters is moderate compared to the stark villainy of Goneril and Regan. The borrowing of themes from Shakespeare draws our attention to an interesting aspect of Balzac's artistic instinct. Between him and the author of *King Lear* there is an affinity which is not only thematic but stylistic, and which can be seen in their combination of tragic and comic elements. This heady mixture of the sublime and the grotesque was an old aesthetic formula which had also been rediscovered by a young generation of French Romantics led by Victor Hugo.

Le Père Goriot had at least two other literary models of which Balzac was certainly conscious, because they are revealed in the text. The first is a novel of education by Fénelon, called *Les Aventures de Télémaque,* which had been published in 1699 but was still much read in the early nineteenth century. Far from hiding the parallel between the experiences of Télémaque and those of Rastignac, Balzac draws attention to it by indicating that the wallpaper in Mme Vauquer's house is decorated with scenes from the old story. In this tale Télémaque receives advice from Mentor, a man of experience who does his best to impart wisdom to the young man. In one episode, however, he cannot prevent him from succumbing to the sexual charms of the nymph Calypso. Télémaque then becomes accustomed to vice and forgets the principles learned in childhood, until Mentor finally does persuade him to leave the dangerous female and the life of easy sensuality and enjoyment she represents. The relationship of Rastignac and Delphine in *Le Père Goriot* therefore reveals itself to be a clever updating and parodic adaptation of this very moral episode in Fénelon's novel. Balzac's other avowed inspiration from the literature of the past was the Greek story of Theseus and Ariadne, an account of ambition, success and ingratitude. In this old tale the legendary Theseus enters the labyrinth and overcomes danger thanks to the help of a princess, just as Rastignac will succeed in Paris with the assistance of a lady of high status. The similarity between the two stories is clearly suggested in a remark made by Mme de Beauséant in *Le Père Goriot* (p.119). Balzac, who was the most modern of writers, knew that real originality did not prevent the use of old structures and familiar themes which had shaped the human imagination since ancient times.

2. The Art of the Novel

Le Père Goriot begins with a dedication to Geoffroy Saint-Hilaire, who had recently established the first Parisian zoo in the Jardin des Plantes. This homage to the well-known zoologist is significant because it reflects Balzac's aspiration to scientific method and precision. Just as the recorder and theorist of the animal world had proceeded by the observation of facts, so will the novelist, it is implied. The first lines of the text, therefore, present themselves as an account of real events in an actual boarding-house in Paris. An unnamed narrator informs us that the establishment still exists, as does its owner Mme Vauquer. Who is this narrator who is at pains to guarantee the accuracy of his account but who does not claim to have been a participant in the events to be related? He tells us he is a student of human nature whose ambition is to record the reality of life in the city of Paris. Far from seeking to speak with the detached and objective manner of a scientist, our narrator and guide has his own opinions which influence the telling of the story, and his character will become familiar to us even though we are never told his name. He announces in the first page that the story is a sad one which will be appreciated mainly by readers who actually know Paris and its callous indifference to individuals. The narrator then speaks directly to an imagined reader, apparently female, who is holding the book in a white hand and sitting in a comfortable armchair, and warns this habitual reader of fiction not to be misled by the title of *Le Père Goriot* into expecting a comic novel about a funny old character called Goriot. In this introductory statement, which has become famous as an example of intervention, the narrator insists on rectifying any such mistaken idea and expresses the fear that the emotional responses of his reader may have been blunted by the exaggerations of contemporary literature. He then urgently claims that the Goriot story has an authenticity which makes it transcend the categories of ordinary fiction: 'Ah! sachez-le: ce drame n'est ni une fiction ni un roman. All is true, il est si véritable que chacun peut en reconnaître les éléments chez soi, dans son cœur peut-être' (p.44) This curious message culminates in an explicit challenge to the reader, urging us to examine our conscience and consider whether we are any better than the selfish characters who act a part in the tragic story of Joachim Goriot.

This intervention by a narrator who lectures an imagined reader is a striking characteristic of the beginning of *Le Père Goriot,* and has inspired much comment in modern times. However, it was not thought exceptional in the age of Balzac, and some knowledge of the literary context in which he was writing is essential for an objective evaluation of his interventionist method. The simple fact is that his first generation of readers recognised this mode as one of the main narrative traditions in the novel. It had already been used in the previous century by famous predecessors like Sterne and Diderot whom Balzac admired, and was still to be found in the works of many contemporary writers, including Stendhal and George Sand. Readers of Balzac therefore accepted it as a familiar mode, and it goes without saying that they could not attempt any anachronistic application of post-Flaubertian criteria to his novels, a fact which gave them an advantage over some modernist critics. The narrator in *Le Père Goriot* plays an intermittent role as a recorder of events and a guide whose task is not to preach morality but to make the reader reflect at times on certain social or psychological realities. An example of this can be seen in his analysis of Rastignac's attraction to Delphine before they have become lovers. Should his desire not be decreased by the fact that there are no great obstacles to overcome and that he knows she is unlikely to resist? Here the narrator intervenes in order to reject this traditional theory and replace it with a different concept of human nature. The male psyche is complex, he asserts, and one aspect of sexual attraction in men is revealed by the case of Rastignac: 'La certitude de réussir engendre mille félicités que les hommes n'avouent pas, et qui font tout le charme de certaines femmes. Le désir ne naît pas moins de la difficulté que de la facilité des triomphes' (p.166). Such comments by the narrator cannot be dismissed as undesirable intrusions in the text since they are relevant to the situation of the fictional character, and add a theoretical dimension to the psychological portrayal. The narrator's observation about Rastignac has the concision and polish of a maxim by La

Rochefoucauld and is a characteristic and valuable part of Balzac's writing.

In *Le Père Goriot* Balzac uses a traditional narrative device by providing information about the alleged sources of information which allowed the story to be written. We are told for example that the narrator learned the facts partly from Rastignac and partly from a certain Muret, who recorded events because of their interest (p.128). Balzac's readers recognised as a familiar convention this use of a main narrator to bring together different strands of a story. It was a method which had long been used by novelists to create an impression of reality, but one notes that Balzac does not persist with this convention in order to explain the narration of events. Instead he seems to decide that the reader is too sophisticated to believe in such artifices and will accept fiction as a serious form of literature which does not need authentification. Muret, the main narrator's alleged assistant and source, is therefore soon eclipsed and forgotten after a few brief mentions of his name. At times a role equivalent to that of narrator is delegated to certain fictional characters such as Mme de Beauséant, Vautrin and Gondureau, all of whom provide important information and also express opinions on social and moral issues. This creates a plurality of viewpoint which is an intrinsic feature of a novel in which authorial opinion is not expressed by the narrator alone (an important subject to which I shall return in a later chapter on the interpretation of themes and meaning). The fact is that narrative perspective in *Le Père Goriot* is not a simple issue, and although at times the voice of the narrator speaks clearly to the reader, there are also many examples of reticence and self-effacement. This can be seen in important episodes where the task of narration is entrusted to fictional characters: Mme de Langeais in her biography of Goriot, Mme de Beauséant in her account of the Goriot daughters, Gondureau in his revelations about Vautrin, and Goriot in his final summary of his life and errors (pp.115, 118, 201, 293). The role given to these characters in the scenes in question is so powerful that the narrator withdraws from the stage, as also happens in the scenes of dialogue which are a frequent and characteristic part of *Le Père Goriot*.

The result is a complexity of perspective which in reality is one of Balzac's typical features. Who is speaking in Balzac's fictional world? It is true that the voice of the narrator is frequently heard, but one cannot say that there is one simple and omniscient narrative perspective which alone represents the opinion of the author. Minor characters contribute to an impression of multiple viewpoint, as can be seen in the episode of Goriot's death where Balzac includes the callous comment of a boarder who does not want his dinner to be delayed: 'Que le père Goriot soit crevé, tant mieux pour lui! Si vous l'adorez, allez le garder, et laissez-nous manger tranquillement, nous autres' (p.309). Balzac then uses the voice of Mme Vauquer to provide another perspective on the sad life of the old man: 'Oh! oui, dit la veuve, tant mieux pour lui qu'il soit mort! Il paraît que le pauvre homme avait bien du désagrément, sa vie durant.' These parodic obituaries for Goriot draw their power from the situation, and Balzac uses them in a manner which interacts with the tragic context. Thus the novelist combines the voices of fictional characters and that of the narrator in a complex orchestration in which the narrator is neither alone nor dominant.

The description of the physical world in *Le Père Goriot* has received almost obsessive attention because of its impact in the first episode, in which Balzac begins with an evocation of the appearance of the area around Mme Vauquer's house and follows it with a detailed account of the establishment itself. These three pages of description written in the present tense precede the narrative. They have probably caused more comment, favourable or hostile, than any other part of the novel, and yet they represent a very small part of the text. They provide a description of the external appearance of the house, including the garden with its geraniums, ivy-covered wall, and the green table under the lime trees where the boarders take their coffee in summer. The novelist adds a back yard containing pigs and other animals, and progresses to the interior of the house which he furnishes with precise detail, including the scenes pictured on the wallpaper, a greasy table and sideboards, stained napkins, and various clocks, artefacts and shabby pieces of furniture. Readers nowadays usually find it difficult to visualise this interior fully, despite the precision of the description. The explanation of this difficulty is the historically specific nature of the setting, which contains objects familiar to readers in 1835, but not to posterity. In spite of this problem the description of Mme Vauquer's house does still gives a strong sense of atmosphere. Balzac's first generation of readers found it both easy to visualise, and an interesting innovation in fiction.

It is to be recalled that Balzac included description not for the sake of novelty, but as part of his ambition to create a scientific type of novel. He believed that any serious writer wishing to be a true observer of contemporary life should not omit the portrayal of the physical world, because it was an integral part of a civilisation. He believed also that a house had significance as an expression of the character of the person who lived in it, and Mme Vauquer and her establishment are portrayed as being inseparable (p.49). One notes that the novelist gives much less description of the homes of the rich than he does of those of the lower classes of society, and those of Mme de Beauséant and of M. de Restaud are left almost entirely to the imagination of the reader. The home of Delphine is briefly described because Balzac considers it to be representative of a new social class and therefore worthy of note: 'Rastignac arriva rue Saint-Lazare, dans une de ces maisons légères, à colonnes minces, à portiques mesquins, qui constituent le *joli* à Paris, une véritable maison de banquier, pleine de recherches coûteuses, des stucs, des paliers d'escalier en mosaïque de marbre. Il trouva Mme de Nucingen dans un petit salon à peintures italiennes, dont le décor ressemblait à celui des cafés' (p.176). Here Balzac is counting on the awareness of a contemporary reader who has actual knowledge of a type of house found in a particular part of the city, and his method is one of referential realism. Conscious of the fact that most of his readers had no difficulty imagining the homes of the rich, Balzac provided much more description of the boarding-house because of its difference. His success can be measured by the fact that the house of Mme Vauquer has acquired legendary status, and his description of it has been carefully studied by generations of literary historians, one of whom has even shown that a brand of wallpaper with scenes from *Télémaque* actually existed at the time. Balzac was the first French novelist to show that such minor aspects of life were worthy of inclusion in literature.

In the physical portrayal of characters too Balzac shows a preference for those who represent low life, as in the vivid portraits of Mme Vauquer, Poiret, Mlle Michonneau, Vautrin and Goriot. Individual portraits of the social élite are less specific, again presumably because they are deemed to be more easily imagined by readers of the class which Balzac had in mind, but Anastasie is described in more detail:

> Rastignac se retourna brusquement et vit la comtesse coquettement vêtue d'un peignoir en cachemire blanc, à nœuds roses, coiffée négligemment, comme le sont les femmes de Paris au matin; elle embaumait, elle avait sans doute pris un bain, et sa beauté, pour ainsi dire assouplie, semblait plus voluptueuse; ses yeux étaient humides. L'œil des jeunes gens sait tout voir: leurs esprits s'unissent aux rayonnements de la femme comme une plante aspire dans l'air des substances qui lui sont propres. Eugène sentit donc la fraîcheur épanouie des mains de cette femme sans avoir besoin d'y toucher. Il voyait, à travers le cachemire, les teintes rosées du corsage que le peignoir, légèrement entrouvert, laissait parfois à nu, et sur lequel son regard s'étalait. (p. 96)

With portraits like this Balzac brought the French novel from the realm of abstraction into that of sensual reality. Anastasie seen through the eager eyes of Rastignac here becomes more than an individual: she is an incarnation of social elegance, of sexual attraction, and of danger. Balzac's evocation of this urban nymph in her dressing-gown is part of his creation of a new mythology of the Parisian world.

Balzac's narrative strategy in *Le Père Goriot* is a traditional one which consists of beginning in the middle of the action, then providing a gradual account of the past events. These are then followed by a series of new events which form a linear narrative leading to an ending. This method had the advantage of being a mode which was familiar to Balzac's readers, and it is also a structure which is close to common experience, since the reader has certainly acquired experience of real people and events in this manner, when information obtained in fragments gradually forms a complete picture. The Goriot story can therefore be described as a narrative and descriptive introduction which is followed by a dramatic development. The main threads of the plot are represented essentially by the individual stories of the major characters, namely Goriot, Vautrin, Rastignac, Delphine, Mme de Beauséant and Anastasie. Balzac combines the destinies of these socially disparate individuals into a coherent web of relationships by his use of the boarding-house as a centre for much of the action. Mme Vauquer's house provides a natural connection between all the protagonists despite their different social spheres, as they are all either residents in it or are linked either to Goriot or to Rastignac.

Another familiar narrative method used here by Balzac is the gradual revelation of hidden facts, a tactic that can be seen in the provision of information about Goriot's past life. The author first gives us the viewpoint of Mme Vauquer and the residents and then intrigues us with various theories about the antecedents and activities of the old man. Where does he go on two evenings in the week, and what is the reason for his financial problems? Has he lost money on the stock market or gambling, or has he spent it on sexual pleasures? We are deliberately led along the wrong path by the novelist when he expounds Mme Vauquer's theory that Goriot is a sexual libertine with costly tastes. Balzac adroitly encourages the reader in this wrong assumption by giving Sylvie's account of a rustling silk dress on the stairs as the old man receives a visit from an expensively dressed young woman. Then another with dark hair comes to see Goriot, and the reader knows no more than the residents, who assume that the mysterious and elegant young persons are paid for their services. Later revelations will show that there is an element of truth in this, but for some time the novelist plays with us. Surely the old man's progressive decline, his move to a cheaper room, confirm the addiction to expensive women? All the facts seem to fit, and the residents, who are well versed in vice, have no reason to doubt Mme Vauquer's logic when she asserts that Goriot would not be living in poverty if he had rich daughters. The novelist adds a further piece of mystery when he places us in the viewpoint of Rastignac spying on the old man and seeing him furtively working on silver plate in the middle of the night. Then Vautrin provides another version of the sexual addiction theory when he asserts that Goriot is the type of man who will destroy himself for his special pleasure. It is not until the account given by Mme de Langeais to Rastignac that Balzac finally ends the mystery and informs the reader that the young females in Goriot's life are indeed his daughters and not his mistresses.

Mystery followed by revelation is also a method used in the narration of Vautrin's life. We ask ourselves how he enters the house despite the locked doors and wonder about his nocturnal activities. Then we learn that Christophe has been approached by a stranger asking questions, and Sylvie too has been interrogated. Balzac tantalises the reader until Inspector Gondureau, who is himself a strange character hiding under a false name, discloses Vautrin's true identity. This systematic use of enigma followed by revelation is a narrative structure which Barthes has called the hermeneutic code, and one which was later to become standard in the *roman policier*. Mystery followed by elucidation can again be seen in the manner in which the financial and personal affairs of Delphine are gradually communicated, as her situation is not fully disclosed until late in the action. Rastignac's role in the plot is often that of investigator. It is he who first learns the facts about Vautrin, Goriot, Delphine and Anastasie, and establishes himself as a solver of riddles and a forerunner of the detective hero in crime fiction.

Scenes of movement and action occur often in *Le Père Goriot*, for example in the episode of Rastignac's first visits to the homes of the aristocracy. We are placed in a physically real world as the young man who cannot afford a cab walks carefully along the muddy streets in an attempt to keep his clothes presentable, but is obliged to stop near the Palais-Royal to have his boots and trousers cleaned. In the courtyard of the house of Count Restaud he sees a thoroughbred horse stamping its hoofs as it waits for its fashionable owner to emerge. Once inside the house Rastignac causes amusement among the servants by barging into a spare room and almost dropping his hat into a bathtub. He is then amazed to hear the voice of old Goriot talking to the elegant Mme de Restaud in a dark corridor, and the sound of a kiss, upon which he moves to a window and looks down on the courtyard in the hope of seeing Goriot leave. When the old man emerges from the building by a side door he unfolds an umbrella, thus startling a horse which has just entered the courtyard, pulling a carriage driven by Count Restaud. More action follows as Rastignac, Maxime, Anastasie and her husband form groups and have discussions. After warning Anastasie not to let herself be courted by Rastignac, Maxime descends to the courtyard where he departs in his elegant carriage, while Anastasie watches from her window.

The novelist then has his young protagonist on the move again as he goes to visit Mme de Beauséant, upon which another detailed account of actions is given. This time he travels in a hired vehicle which will protect him from the rain and project an image of prosperity, and we see him throw his hat on the front seat and settle proudly in the carriage. But his satisfaction is shortlived when the great doors of the Beauséant property open with a groan and admit him to a courtyard where his inappropriate vehicle draws repressed titters from a new set of servants and he observes a carriage even more splendid than that of Maxime. We follow his progress through a glass door and up a grand red carpeted staircase full of flowers, and when Rastignac is admitted to the presence of his cousin, Balzac introduces d'Ajuda Pinto, a new character who uses Rastignac's arrival as a pretext for his own departure. Mme de Beauséant then runs to a window to hear what destination is given to the driver, discovers that her lover has not told her the truth, and writes him a note with a trembling hand. The theatrical character of this scene full of events is prolonged when Balzac introduces Mme de Langeais, who is greeted with affectionate physical gestures by Mme de Beauséant. An important dialogue then takes place between the two women, whose facial expressions are indicated in the manner of stage directions.

The narrative of the action continues as Balzac recounts Rastignac's return to the Latin quarter where he goes upstairs to his room and then down again with money to pay the driver. The detailed account of Rastignac's progress between the miserable boarding-house and the homes of the rich has significance because it is the story of a voyage of discovery during which the young man sees sights and acquires experience which will change his attitude, and ultimately transform his life. To these two hours in the life of

Rastignac Balzac has devoted an episode full of movement as his youthful adventurer advances through life in the manner of a picaresque hero.

Action of a more dramatic sort is found in the episode of Vautrin's arrest, which begins with the sound of a cab outside the house and of hurried footsteps which precede the entry of a servant bringing news of the killing of Victorine's brother (p.224). Rastignac reacts with shock while Vautrin calmly drinks coffee, not knowing that it is drugged. He then loses consciousness and is carried upstairs where his shirt is removed by the treacherous Michonneau in order to look for the marks which will show him to be a branded criminal. The police suddenly arrive and Gondureau tears off Vautrin's wig to reveal his real face, upon which the unmasked criminal dramatically quits the stage after a last defiant speech. Thus ends an episode in which Balzac deliberately and skilfully performs the time-honoured role of the novelist as a narrator of exciting events.

A significant part of the narrative method used in *Le Père Goriot* is the creation of suspense, for example in the Vautrin story. At an early point in the narrative we are told that questions are being asked about this character by unknown individuals who try to draw information firstly from Christophe, then from Sylvie, Poiret and Michonneau. The dialogue between Gondureau and Michonneau then heightens the tension, as we wait for her to decide which person she will betray (p.203). The relationship between Rastignac and Delphine also creates much expectation and uncertainty. What are the real thoughts of Delphine when he makes his first declaration? Is her husband aware of her adultery, and what will be his reaction if he finds out? When will she give herself to Rastignac? Just as Delphine makes Rastignac wait for the moment of pleasure, so Balzac makes his reader be patient and await the outcome.

A very strong use of suspense is evident in the episode of Goriot's illness when he waits in the hope of seeing his daughters one last time. The announcement that the old man is doomed coincides with the anxiety and excitement of the approaching ball at which Anastasie is to display the Restaud diamonds and Delphine will make her much awaited entry into the closed circle of the aristocracy. In these pages Balzac enhances the sense of passing time and urgency, while Goriot vainly waits (pp.287-313). In a final use of suspense the novelist carefully prolongs Rastignac's own agony, and the hesitation before his choice of a route in life. The young man's indignation in the harrowing scenes of Goriot's abandonment cleverly encourages us to think that he will now stop seeing Delphine, and as we read the account of him standing in the cemetery and reflecting on the sadness of life, we wonder what precise form his rejection of her will take. The novelist then surprises and confounds the reader by making Rastignac go to dine with Delphine that very evening. The decision which determines his future life has been postponed until the very last line of the novel, as Balzac gives one final demonstration of his ability to create dramatic suspense and involve the imagination of his expectant reader.

Another of Balzac's narrative skills is seen in the management of scenes of dialogue, a good example being the discussion which takes place between Bianchon and Rastignac, when the latter is on the verge of agreeing to the killing of young Taillefer and wants to hear his friend's opinion without arousing his suspicion:

> As-tu lu Rousseau ?
> —Oui.
> —Te souviens-tu de ce passage où il demande à son lecteur ce qu'il ferait au cas où il pourrait s'enrichir en tuant à la Chine par sa seule volonté un vieux mandarin, sans bouger de Paris.
> —Oui.
> —Eh bien?
> —Bah! J'en suis à mon trente-troisième mandarin.
> —Ne plaisante pas. Allons, s'il t'était prouvé que la chose est possible et qu'il te suffit d'un signe de tête, le ferais-tu?
> —Est-il bien vieux, le mandarin? Mais, bah! jeune ou vieux, paralytique ou bien portant, ma foi...Diantre! Eh bien, non.   (pp.171-72)

Here a deadly serious moral discussion is woven into a superficially amusing dialogue in which Bianchon, who speaks with the voice of simple honesty, is elevated into a figure of symbolic importance.

There is another striking use of direct speech in the scene in which Vautrin assesses Rastignac's situation and speaks with Balzac's most colourful style, as if he had a liberating effect on the novelist's imagination: 'C'est fatigant de désirer toujours sans jamais se satisfaire. Si vous étiez pâle et de la nature des mollusques, vous n'auriez rien à craindre; mais nous avons le sang fiévreux des lions et un appétit à faire vingt sottises par jour' (p.142). This long speech full of animal and sexual imagery shows Balzac enthusiastically suspending the principles of good taste as he revels in the vivid language of low life.

Balzac's powerful use of direct speech can also be seen in Goriot's last outburst to Rastignac. The dying man has just learned that his daughters are not coming to see him and the novelist makes him speak with dramatic eloquence:

> Ah! si j'étais riche, si j'avais gardé ma fortune, si je ne la leur avais pas donnée, elles seraient là, elles me lécheraient les joues de leurs baisers! je demeurerais dans un hôtel, j'aurais de belles chambres, des domestiques, du feu à moi; et elles seraient tout en larmes, avec leurs maris, leurs enfants. J'aurais tout cela. Mais rien. L'argent donne tout, même des filles.
>
> (pp.293-94)

A feature of this final speech by Goriot is its considerable length, which increases its impact. The old man's dying words, which fluctuate between contradictory sentiments, are a piece of stylistic virtuosity in which Balzac shows his ability to write emotively while avoiding the facile pathos often found in the death-bed scenes of earlier novelists.

A less dramatic aspect of his stylistic skill is provided by the epistolary mode which is introduced with the letters from Rastignac's mother and sister (pp.129-33). Here too the form of expression strongly suggests the different personalities of the writers: playful and cheerful in the case of Laure; anxious and poignant in the case of Mme Rastignac. The ability to make different characters speak with individual voices is essential for a novelist and Balzac possessed it in high degree, as can be seen in the conversations of the residents of

Mme Vauquer's house. Their voices vividly evoke the popular culture of early nineteenth century Paris with their references to contemporary plays and other entertainments like the diorama. Balzac's skill in making characters speak has given literary immortality even to minor figures who seem to transcend fiction and become a piece of living cultural history.

It is not difficult to find fault with certain aspects of Balzac's style or to highlight occasional examples of verbosity, but such lapses are rare in *Le Père Goriot*. Often the Balzacian metaphor has great concision and power, and the theme of animal characteristics runs strongly through a series of images. Mlle Michonneau for example has the eyes of a viper and Vautrin's roar of anger is like that of a lion. Another group of metaphors is sexually suggestive, which explains the censorious reactions of some early critics of Balzac's style. 'Le mors est mis à ma bête, sautons dessus et gouvernons-la' (p.164): this brutal image is used by Rastignac as he begins his courtship of Delphine. D'Ajuda-Pinto, when he comments on the young man's impure intentions regarding the banker's wife, says: 'Il va faire sauter la banque. Il est souple comme une anguille, et je crois qu'il ira loin' (ibid.). Vautrin too uses a sexual image when he urges Rastignac to seduce Victorine: 'Poussons chacun nos pointes! La mienne est en fer et ne mollit jamais, hé, hé!' (p. 197). Mme Vauquer's comment to Rastignac on his relationship with Victorine is an equally indecent play on words: 'Dites donc, monsieur Eugène (...), vous avez mis la main au bon endroit' (p.225). Balzac's style is a highly individual and original linguistic form which covers a broad and colourful spectrum.

While considering the structure of the Goriot story it is essential not to exaggerate the function of the narrator. It is evident that he does at times play an openly explanatory role, but there are important parts of the text in which an act of interpretation is expected from the reader without any comment from the narrator. We see this when Anastasie talks about Maxime, and unconsciously reveals the method used by her lover to maintain his hold over her:

Vers le commencement de janvier, M. de Trailles me
paraissait bien chagrin. Il ne me disait rien; mais il est si

facile de lire dans le cœur des gens qu'on aime, un rien
suffit: puis il y a des pressentiments. Enfin il était plus
aimant, plus tendre que je ne l'avais jamais vu, j'étais
toujours plus heureuse. Pauvre Maxime! dans sa pensée,
il me faisait ses adieux, m'a-t-il dit; il voulait se brûler la
cervelle. Enfin je l'ai tant tourmenté, tant supplié, je suis
restée deux heures à ses genoux. Il m'a dit qu'il devait
cent mille francs! Oh! papa, cent mille francs! Je suis
devenue folle. (p. 262)

In these lines the novelist withholds the thoughts of the narrator, and
instead gives us the illusions of Anastasie. These are presented in a
natural and unelucidated state, the reader being expected to work
things out without explanation. A similar example of authorial
discretion can be observed in the important last scene when
Rastignac remains alone in the graveyard after Goriot's funeral:

Rastignac, resté seul, fit quelques pas vers le haut du
cimetière et vit Paris tortueusement couché le long des
deux rives de la Seine, où commençaient à briller les
lumières. Ses yeux s'attachèrent presque avidement entre
la colonne de la place Vendôme et le dôme des Invalides,
là où vivait ce beau monde dans lequel il avait voulu
pénétrer. Il lança sur cette ruche bourdonnante un regard
qui semblait par avance en pomper le miel, et dit ces
mots grandioses: «A nous deux maintenant!».
Et pour premier acte du défi qu'il portait à la Société,
Rastignac alla dîner chez Mme de Nucingen

(pp.312-13)

This famous conclusion has such concision that it borders on the
enigmatic. It requires a considerable effort of interpretation by the
reader, who must seek the implications of the decision made by
Rastignac. What is the exact nature of this alleged challenge to
Society, and what does the future hold for Delphine and him after his
latest experience of her character? The novelist has closed the
personal story of Joachim Goriot with dramatic finality, but the
destiny of these other major characters remains unrevealed. The

ending has the appearance of a new beginning, since it possesses the Gidean quality of a story which can be continued. Balzac ends his narrative with a note of authorial reticence, and stimulates the imagination of the reader with a final element of mystery and suspense.

3. Characters

When Balzac began his writing career, more than a decade before *Le Père Goriot*, the main characters in serious French novels were usually members of the aristocracy whose lives were remote from prosaic concerns such as money and the practicalities of daily life. Balzac did more than any other French novelist of his time to depart from this tradition, although some of his novels do have aristocratic protagonists. In his portrayal of middle-class characters and his inclusion of domestic servants and occasional representatives of the working class, his intention was to broaden the social spectrum of fiction. By increasing the role of characters not drawn from the aristocracy, he was also following the example of the comic novels of his admired predecessors Fielding, Sterne and Diderot. The characters in *Le Père Goriot* come from the fusion of two fictional traditions, one serious and one comic, and a part of Balzac's originality lies in this blending of contrasting elements.

His characters are also founded on theoretical principles which were made explicit in an *Avant-propos* written in 1842 for his collected works. One of these was a belief in the essential unity of the world of animals and that of humans, an idea inspired by Geoffroy Saint-Hilaire and his theory that all animals are engaged in a struggle to survive, and that successful individuals evolve in order to adapt to different environments. Balzac's addition was the idea that Society resembles Nature, and that different social environments have created a variety of human species which are as unlike each other as wolves and sheep. The belief in the similarity between the world of humans and that of animals gave Balzac the ambition to portray all aspects of French society as the great zoologist Buffon had described the whole animal world. His study would be scientific in the sense that it would be methodical, comprehensive, and include the fascinating and neglected subject of human artefacts: 'l'œuvre à faire devait avoir une triple forme: les hommes, les femmes et les choses, c'est-à-dire les personnes et la représentation matérielle qu'ils donnent de leur pensée; enfin, l'homme et la vie' (*1*, I, p.10).

Balzac's ambition was also to provide a new sort of historical record of French society in the first decades of the nineteenth century in order to compensate for the deficiency of official historians, who concerned themselves only with records of major events and neglected those facts of everyday life which he called *l'histoire des mœurs*. Whereas previous French novelists had not provided their characters with significant physical features, Balzac wanted his own readers to visualise Goriot precisely with his blue coat, white waistcoat and gold chain. We are told of his habit of sniffing his bread; we know his cold, damp room with its loose wallpaper and shabby furniture; we become familiar with his voice, with the expressions on his face, and the physical signs of his financial decline. The figure of Goriot has historical significance as a representation of a section of French society which made a fortune in the Revolution of 1789. Goriot started life as an uneducated manual worker employed by a Parisian flour-merchant and when this member of the middle class became a victim of the Revolution, he purchased the business cheaply. Goriot's upward mobility had started and his obscurity and mediocrity allowed him to survive a dangerous period during which he became rich owing to his commercial position in a time of food shortages. In France after the Revolution there was an erosion of social barriers which made it easy for the wealthy Goriot to marry one daughter with a member of the old French nobility, and the other with a representative of the new financial aristocracy. Soon tension existed between the commoner father and his daughters, who found themselves on the other side of a class barrier which was once again asserting itself. In this way Goriot's individual story is interwoven with the history of French society during a period of fluctuation and exceptional social mobility.

In psychological terms the character of Goriot is a curious combination of lucidity and blindness. His rise in society indicates energy, judgment, foresight, shrewdness and competence, but his private life shows a lack of elementary intelligence, as he gives extravagant habits to his daughters and allows them to be selfish and superficial. Although his family has disintegrated he will not face reality: 'Les deux sœurs se jalousent, voyez-vous? c'est encore une preuve de leur tendresse. Mme de Restaud m'aime bien aussi. Je le sais. Un père est avec ses enfants comme Dieu est avec nous, il va jusqu'au fond des cœurs, et juge les intentions. Elles sont toutes deux aussi aimantes' (p.167). Even when the sisters exchange vicious insults he stills thinks they are angelic, and cannot see that they are using him without scruple. Yet Goriot remains perceptive in other matters, quickly penetrating Nucingen's plot to steal Delphine's dowry and his dishonest explanations: 'Et tu crois à ces sornettes, s'écria le père Goriot. C'est un comédien! J'ai rencontré des Allemands en affaires: ces gens-là sont presque tous de bonne foi, pleins de candeur; mais quand, sous leur air de franchise et de bonhomie, ils se mettent à être malins et charlatans, ils le sont alors plus que les autres' (p.257). Goriot is naïve in all matters concerning his daughters, apparently unaware of their manipulation of him and submissive to their demands. He is capable of self-abasement, lying at Delphine's feet and fawning on her like a dog.

In addition, his bizarre behaviour is more than once compared to that of a lover, and Balzac stresses the unnatural attitude of Goriot to daughters whom he treats like kept mistresses. His knowledge of Delphine's sex-life is detailed and intimate, and he is tormented by the thought that she has not had pleasure with her husband. His attachment to her is strongly physical and his language is that of a lover: 'Est-ce bon de se frotter à sa robe, de se mettre à son pas, de partager sa chaleur!' (p.209). In a moment of happiness he squeezes her so violently that he hurts her, and the thought of sexual relations between Delphine and her husband gives him homicidal thoughts. Thus Balzac indicates the distortion of a paternal love carried to excess, a fact which Goriot himself will finally admit: 'Mes filles, c'était mon vice à moi; elles étaient mes maîtresses, enfin tout!' (p.295). The logic and coherence of Goriot's character lies in a transfer of affection from his dead wife to his daughters. A widowed Goriot with sons would have been a different character, and here lies the key to an original psychological study in which gender is an essential factor, and in which Goriot's behaviour shows a sublimation of frustrated conjugal love.

The complexity of Goriot's psyche is again shown in the cleverly conceived final speech when Christophe has revealed that neither of his daughters is coming to see him before he dies. A lesser novelist than Balzac might have had the old man once again finding excuses for the young women, but he surprises us with the revelation of an inner lucidity in Goriot. It is implied that in a part of his mind he has always known the truth about their character and his situation but refused to admit it, and at this point Balzac makes the old man face reality in a tragic moment of recognition:

> —Aucune de ses filles ne viendrait, s'écria Rastignac. Je vais écrire à toutes deux.
> —Aucune, répondit le vieillard en se dressant sur son séant. Elles ont des affaires, elles dorment, elles ne viendront pas. Je le savais. Il faut mourir pour savoir ce que c'est que des enfants. Ah! mon ami, ne vous mariez pas, n'ayez pas d'enfants! Vous leur donnez la vie, ils vous donnent la mort. Vous les faites entrer dans le monde, ils vous en chassent. Non, elles ne viendront pas! Je sais cela depuis dix ans. Je me le disais quelque-fois, mais je n'osais pas y croire. (p.293)

The depth of the character is finally demonstrated in this fine episode, in which the author creates true pathos. The figure of Goriot, which is historically significant as a portrayal of the evolution of French society after the Revolution, is also a coherent, subtle and highly original psychological study of excessive paternal love, and an eloquent demonstration of Balzac's ability to create a memorable character.

The question of the exact status of Rastignac in *Le Père Goriot* is an interesting one, since it is possible to argue that he is the real protagonist. We see most events through his eyes, and he interacts progressively with all the main characters including Mme de Beauséant, Vautrin, Delphine and Goriot himself. The role of Rastignac, as the old man's friend and as Delphine's lover, is so closely linked to Goriot's life that it becomes an intimate part of it. It can therefore be said that this novel is a tight web of individual lives in which the destinies of Goriot and Rastignac are dominant strands. It is an account of Goriot's fall and of Rastignac's rise; a story of delusion and of lucidity; the history of an ending and of a beginning. Whereas Goriot's fictional career concludes with the finality of death, that of Rastignac is destined to continue.

Rastignac resembles the typical protagonist in the traditional French novel in that he is young, attractive, aristocratic, talented and engaged in an apprenticeship of life, and from Des Grieux (in Prévost's *Manon Lescaut*) to him the literary lineage is direct. Balzac's introduction of the character outlines the features which make him into what the novelist calls a type, which means that he is conceived as a representation of recognisable human categories, though credible as an individual. In his psychological dimension Rastignac is a representation of the young male eager for experience and success, and in his external characteristics he personifies the ambitious young provincials in Paris who were part of a new social mobility in the early nineteenth century. The pages devoted to Eugène provide a geographical framework by the evocation of his provincial background on a farm near Angoulême (pp.71-72). A large part of the family income is invested in sending Eugène to study law in Paris, and little remains for his relatives who have to scrimp and save to keep up the respectable appearance expected from landed gentry. Rastignac himself leads a financially restricted life in Paris, and Balzac paints a vivid picture of the student hunched over his law books in his shabby room as he tries to warm himself in front of a miserable fire.

The portrait of Rastignac gives an account of his mental and emotional development over a period of about two years, the main action beginning when he has returned to Paris for his second session of law studies. At this point he has already abandoned his first plan to achieve success by hard work and personal merit alone. He is now tempted to use the family name in order to get into high society and make useful contacts with influential women. Balzac shows Rastignac's state of mind after his first experience of aristocratic life at Mme de Beauséant's ball. The impact of the experience is profound, and his former idealistic intention to succeed by personal merit is now swept away by a new awareness of the life led by the social élite. The young man's feelings are portrayed with realism when Rastignac, who is no undersexed young hero from a sentimental novel, dances with Anastasie and desires her 'formes pleines et rondes' (p.74). With these details Balzac introduces us into a world which is not divorced from carnal reality, and he also evocatively portrays the workings of the mind as Rastignac looks into the fire and imagines details of a future love-affair with Anastasie.

The comic side of Rastignac's situation and attitude is revealed in these early episodes of his social education, and we see it in his blundering visit to the home of Anastasie and also when he first meets Delphine, imagining that he has completely charmed her. Much of his courtship of Delphine shows this inexperience and passivity, for example when she gives him money and sends him to play roulette for her. A temporary reversal of gender roles is indicated by a metaphor when she wants to give him some of the winnings, and he resists 'comme une vierge' (p.182), but ends up by accepting the money. The devirilisation of the young man is continued by her refusal to give sexual favours, and his passivity persists as he accepts expensive presents. The process culminates in the gift of an apartment, which will be Delphine's place of pleasure (p.242). The manipulation of Rastignac by Vautrin is another example of his early passivity, since it is the older man who proposes, plans, and acts. Eugène's role is once again to be courted, tempted, and persuaded, the metaphor of virginity recurring when he is compared to a girl who is considering selling herself if the price is right (p.155).

This account of Rastignac's inexperience places the character firmly in the tradition of the education novel, since he personifies youthful decency in contact with the wicked ways of the world. His mind is like a stage upon which a moral drama is acted out before our eyes, the voice of virtue being represented partly by his mother. Her letter of advice to Eugène provides a code of wise and honest principles: do not frequent people richer than yourself; do not try to appear what you are not; crooked paths do not lead to great achievement; hard work and patience are the necessary virtues of the poor (pp.129-30). The sensitive and principled young man is well aware of the sacrifice made by his family so that he can obtain a professional qualification. Their hope is that he will be able to help them in return, and he knows the urgency of the situation, as suitable husbands for his sisters cannot be found without money for a dowry.

His intentions are excellent: he will study hard, find some lucrative position and repay his family. But when the difficulty of achieving anything by merit and patience is revealed to him, he becomes receptive to the influence of Vautrin, who clarifies his situation as one in which he must quickly choose between honesty, corruption and crime.

Rastignac's instinct makes him favour honesty, but he sees it to be slow and ineffective. On the other hand crime appears rapid and effective, but is contrary to principles which are deeply rooted in him because of his upbringing. Time, however, will prove the power of temptation, and Rastignac listens attentively to Vautrin's proposal of a quick fortune which involves a criminal act (pp.148-50). When he learns the details of the plan, he at first rejects it. But then the seed sown by Vautrin quickly germinates, and the day comes when the young man is ready to participate in the plot which will lead to the killing of Victorine's brother, and the change in her father's will. After the killing takes place he is affected by the shock of realisation, and draws back from the association with Vautrin. He knows that he is morally involved in the crime and at this point wants to extricate himself. Balzac portrays his troubled conscience in a manner which is subtle and sympathetic. Vautrin, in his valedictory speech to the residents of the boarding-house, describes Rastignac as 'le meilleur d'entre vous' (p.233), and no doubt this is Balzac's own assessment of the young protagonist.

The novelist also gives a refined and detailed analysis of Rastignac's mind and emotions during the development of his love for Delphine. The relationship has a profound influence on his life, since he quickly becomes addicted to the attractive and more experienced woman. Though he is not blind to her frivolity and selfishness, he has not got the courage to influence her behaviour or the strength to stop seeing her. He engages in self-deception, persuading himself that there are special circumstances, that she is not so bad after all and that she will finally do something for her father. It is when this illusion can no longer be maintained that Rastignac ends his hesitation and silences the voice of conscience. He now sees that Delphine is more selfish than he ever feared, and makes the decision that he will continue to be her lover, and will learn to use others ruthlessly. This is an act of calculation and of moral compromise, but Balzac still portrays him with under-standing: his conflict has been real; the situation is a complex one; his method is immoral but his intentions are good. Future events will show that he does help his family and provide dowries for his sisters.

If Balzac's characters can be divided into winners and losers, it is clear that Rastignac is one of the former, as is indicated symbolically when he plays roulette and fills his pockets with gold. With his highly individual character and interesting situation, he is justly famous as one of Balzac's finest creations. There is no more captivating psychological portrayal in the Goriot story than the figure of Rastignac, as we follow the progress of the young man's noble aspirations, and observe his final surrender to expediency.

The character of Delphine was not what was expected by readers of traditional novels, which often portrayed a superior woman experiencing disappointment in love. Delphine's social and psychological situation makes her startlingly different from these idealised figures since she has freely chosen a husband for his money and then refused to accept responsibility for the consequences. She is a social climber who coldly neglects the father who has sacrificed so much for her. She is reckless, careless of her dignity, ready to compromise herself with Rastignac before she knows him, telling him the secrets of her marriage, sending him to gamble her money in order to repay her former lover. Again, she accepts no personal blame for her situation but claims that everything is the fault of her husband, or of her father for letting him marry her. She explains to Rastignac that her debts are a minor mistake which she attributes to youthful inexperience, not to her own extravagance. She accepted money from Henri de Marsay, but is it not natural to share with the person you love, she asks? The situation became embarrassing only when he left her without justification, she claims. As for her husband, she tells Rastignac that she finds him physically repulsive and refuses all sexual contact with him. In a self-portrait which shows shameless indulgence and a total lack of lucidity, Delphine presents herself as a touching and faultless victim of father, husband and lover (pp.180-82).

An interesting feature of the character of Delphine is her energy, a quality often found in Balzac's major figures. Having been jilted by one lover and having received the insincere and calculating courtship of another, she turns the situation to her advantage. Here the novelist gives a detailed and amusing analysis of a situation in which her skill in sexual tactics soon gives her power over Rastignac. Because of her flirtatious overtures Delphine has compromised herself in the eyes of high society, which soon believes that he has already filled the space left by Henri de Marsay. In reality she is making him wait, and applying a deliberate policy which is successfully producing a stronger attachment: 'Depuis un mois elle irritait si bien les sens d'Eugène, qu'elle avait fini par attaquer le cœur' (p.191). Tentatively exploring the psyche of Delphine, the narrator speaks as if she were a living person and debates the question of her intentions: is she just a coquette, or are deeper emotions involved? He answers by explaining that Delphine's behaviour is partly due to an instinctive female hesitation before accepting a lover, and also to a desire to regain some of her dignity. After a degrading sexual experience, she was now enjoying for the first time the sensation of an old-fashioned courtship with holding of hands and occasional kisses.

Balzac narrates this stage in Delphine's love-affair with finesse, originality and humour in the episode where Delphine persuades Rastignac that he can honourably accept the gift of an apartment and the status of kept lover. Did ladies in olden times not make gifts of armour to the young knight who would wear their ribbon in the tournament, she asks? The weapons of the chivalrous past have been replaced by the finery of the modern dandy: 'les choses que je vous offre sont les armes de l'époque, des outils nécessaires à qui veut être quelque chose' (p.244). Principles of honour decree that a gentleman should not be kept by a lady, but they get short shrift from Delphine. This highly unconventional female protagonist does have a link with more traditional fictional heroines in the form of her aspiration to a certain type of happiness. In his account of her discovery of emotional and sexual satisfaction, Balzac briefly raises Delphine to a higher plane and makes her speak with the eloquence of sentimental love:

> Il n'est plus aujourd'hui qu'une seule crainte, un seul malheur pour moi, c'est de perdre l'amour qui m'a fait

> sentir le plaisir de vivre. En dehors de ce sentiment tout
> m'est indifférent, je n'aime plus rien au monde. Vous
> êtes tout pour moi. Si je sens le bonheur d'être riche,
> c'est pour mieux vous plaire. Je suis, à ma honte, plus
> amante que je ne suis fille. Pourquoi? je ne sais. Toute
> ma vie est en vous. Mon père m'a donné un cœur, mais
> vous l'avez fait battre. (p.273)

Balzac nevertheless remains consistent in his portrait of a woman
whose selfish nature has not changed, and his ironical use of
uncommented direct speech is eloquent in Delphine's response to
Rastignac's urging her to see her sick father: 'Eh bien, oui, dit-elle,
mais après le bal. Mon bon Eugène, sois gentil, ne me fais pas de
morale, viens' (p.282). She sheds a rapid tear for Goriot, but soon
wipes it away when she reflects that such emotions would ruin her
appearance at the ball, and she fobs Rastignac off with an insincere
promise that she will soon go to her father. Thus Balzac completes
his portrait of an individual who is neither angel nor villain; a woman
disappointed by marriage and who seeks emotional satisfaction in
adultery; a woman of experience who chooses a younger man. The
novelty and fascination of the character of Delphine for Balzac's
female readers are easy to perceive.

Whereas the interest of figures like Rastignac and Delphine is
explained by their close links with common experience, that of
Vautrin lies elsewhere. No French novelist before Balzac had
attempted such a serious and sympathetic portrayal of a homosexual,
and Vautrin towers over the caricatural sodomites in the novels of
Sade just as he overshadows the coy aesthetes of Gide. Balzac's
originality is also evident in his portrayal of a professional criminal,
which is one of the rarest human types to be found in literature, and
his achievement can be measured by a comparison with the crudely
drawn figure of Fagin in Dickens's *Oliver Twist*. Balzac's portrayal
of Vautrin's sexual tendency is subtle and coded, and is tinged with
humour in the use of the theme-song in which the homosexual quotes
the amorous hero of a contemporary comic opera:

> *J'ai longtemps parcouru le monde,*
> *Et l'on m'a vu de toute part,*

Courtiser la brune et la blonde
Aimer, soupirer au hasard (p.80)

Vautrin's homosexuality is suggested by his expressions of affection
for Rastignac, but the latter does not understand all the reasons why
the older man is proposing an association. At one point Vautrin hints
at future revelation of a secret which cannot be said aloud: 'Vous
vous demandez pourquoi ce dévouement? Eh bien, je vous le dirai
tout doucement quelque jour, dans le tuyau de l'oreille' (p.195). He
is attracted to Rastignac by the qualities which make him different
from himself: his youth, good looks, honesty and heterosexuality. He
does not seek physical contact and his affection expresses itself in a
manner which alternates between the language of courtship and that
of paternity. Rastignac always remains unaware of the older man's
sexual inclination and does not understand the complex nature of his
motivation in proposing the pact between them. Vautrin, it is implied,
will satisfy himself with a partnership which is based on friendship
and loyalty. His affection excludes jealousy and he is ready to take
pleasure in Rastignac's future success with women. When the
criminal is about to quit the scene he adopts 'une voix douce et triste'
in his farewell to his young friend, and thus Balzac completes his
original and sympathetic portrayal of the love which dared not speak
its name.

Unlike Dickens with the odious Fagin, Balzac endows Vautrin
with superior qualities such as energy, self-reliance and generosity.
His ambition for Rastignac is to establish the young man as a
privileged prince among thieves:

> Ah! si vous vouliez devenir mon élève, je vous ferais
> arriver à tout. Vous ne formeriez pas un désir qu'il ne fût
> à l'instant comblé, quoi que vous puissiez souhaiter:
> honneur, fortune, femmes. On vous réduirait toute la
> civilisation en ambroisie. Vous seriez notre enfant gâté,
> notre Benjamin, nous nous exterminerions tous pour
> vous avec plaisir. (p.194)

In Balzac's account of the temptation of Rastignac there are allusions
to Satan and Mephistopheles, and an awareness of myth, but
essentially there is nothing supernatural in Vautrin. In the end he is

caught as a consequence of a very human error, the over-confidence which leads him to make an enemy of Michonneau. It is true that in the character of Vautrin the novelist does go beyond the frontier of narrowly conceived realism, and by doing so creates one of those exceptional figures which fascinated the Romantic imagination.

Mme de Beauséant for her part is a less original literary character, being a touching victim of life who has links with traditional fictional models such as Richardson's Clarissa. There are pages in which Balzac goes perilously close to idealisation of this female character, though he does finally contribute an interesting variant of the conventional theme of a superior woman disappointed in love. The situation of Mme de Beauséant is not explained solely by the lack of commitment in her lover, but reveals certain harsh realities which are cruelly explained by Mme de Langeais: a woman who loves too much can tire a man with her emotional demands; one should control and hide affection; the power of society over irregular relationships is strong; happiness in love tends not to last.

As well as expressing these important themes, the case of Mme de Beauséant is used by Balzac to formulate a criticism of high society, since she describes the women in her social circle as frivolous, hypocritical and vicious (pp.117-19). She tells Rastignac that if he wants to succeed he must use people without scruple, and strike without pity, and she ripostes with deadly sarcasm when her best friend eagerly brings the news that her lover is deceiving her. In the final episode of Mme de Beauséant's emotional drama, when she is about to leave Paris for ever, Balzac lapses briefly into a sentimental mode and compares her to illustrious females in myth and history (pp.283-84). She goes to hide herself in the country with the intention of devoting the rest of her life to solitude and melancholy, because she mistakenly believes that a woman like herself can love only once. Ultimately Balzac does not portray Mme de Beauséant as a personification of virtue and innocence, as if she were the heroine of some sentimental novel, but as a woman who expects too much from men, and who suffers the consequences of her error.

Balzac's major characters can be seen as a representation of certain themes: paternity in Goriot, crime in Vautrin, sentiment in

Mme de Beauséant, ambition in Rastignac. However, any attempt to
define them in such simple terms can only be approximate and
reductive, given their complexity. Similarly Balzac's remarkable
theory, according to which human individuals belong to species
which are as different as wolves and sheep, does not reduce the aura
of individuality produced by his characters. We judge his fictional
world not in scientific but in literary terms, and Balzac's animal
theory gives his characters a hidden dimension which explains part of
their impact on the imagination. He sees personality as an essence
and, although individuals in his novels may be influenced by people
and by circumstance, they are born with a character which will not
change. Vautrin will always be the same and so will Mme de
Beauséant, destined by Nature to be a winner or a loser.

The minor characters in *Le Père Goriot* also form an important
part of Balzac's fictional world. Impressive in their diversity, they
form a large group which extends from the servants Sylvie and
Christophe to the banker Nucingen and the aristocratic Restaud. We
have already observed the stylistic skill with which Balzac
differentiates between the speech of members of the different classes.
His use of dialogue is an important part of the characterisation of
figures such as Bianchon, Poiret and Gondureau. Metaphor too is
used with striking effect in the portrayal of minor characters, for
example when the bony frame of Mlle Michonneau inspires Vautrin
to call her a 'Vénus du Père-Lachaise' (p.212), a nickname which
suggests the skeletal female figures symbolising death which were to
be found on tombstones in the old cemetery. Balzac does not follow
the tradition of the comic novel in which writers such as Paul de
Kock portrayed lower-class individuals as essentially amusing
figures. On the contrary, those who reside in Mme Vauquer's house
have a cruel nature which takes pleasure in persecuting a harmless
old man. Balzac's achievement as a creator of characters is historic in
the sense that it has left a lasting mark on French culture, since the
names of Rastignac, Goriot and Vautrin have entered the national
consciousness and become a part of the language. Even minor figures
such as Mme Vauquer and her cat Mistigris have lived in the
imagination of generations of readers, unlike the pale figures in
novels by so many contemporaries of Balzac.

4. Themes

In *Le Père Goriot* and in earlier works Balzac explored a number of themes which had been neglected or less fully exploited by French novelists of the previous generation, and which included commerce, money, class, social evolution, and city life. Beside these relatively new themes stood the old ones of love and marriage, which were one of the main foundations of fiction. Novels in which love featured prominently tended to divide into two categories: firstly there were those with an account of a courtship which overcomes obstacles and leads to a happy end; secondly there were those with a tragic conclusion, a type of story preferred by many of the greater novelists, from Prévost to Stendhal. *Le Père Goriot* contains a situation which offers the chance of a love-story with a happy ending, if Rastignac had fallen in love with Victorine, and married her. The narrator draws attention to this possible outcome and briefly pays tribute to a type of fiction which he will choose not to imitate:

> Pauvre fille! un serrement de mains, sa joue effleurée par les cheveux de Rastignac, une parole dite si près de son oreille qu'elle avait senti la chaleur des lèvres de l'étudiant, la pression de sa taille par un bras tremblant, un baiser pris sur son cou, furent les accordailles de sa passion, que le voisinage de la grosse Sylvie, menaçant de rentrer dans cette radieuse salle à manger, rendirent plus ardentes, plus vives, plus engageantes que les plus beaux témoignages racontés dans les plus célèbres histoires d'amour. (p.206)

Balzac then returns to his own unsentimental theme, which is expressed firstly by Mme de Beauséant's failure in love. Her relationship with d'Ajuda-Pinto is in crisis owing to his family's desire for him to marry, and Balzac focuses on the problems of a love-affair which is subjected to social pressure and undermined by deception, since her lover himself wishes to break free. The interesting situation leads Mme de Langeais to formulate a general theory of love and rejection, one which applies to Goriot as it does to Mme de Beauséant:

> Ce qui arrive à ce père peut arriver à la plus jolie femme
> avec l'homme qu'elle aimera le mieux: si elle l'ennuie de
> son amour, il s'en va, il fait des lâchetés pour la fuir.
> Tous les sentiments en sont là. Notre cœur est un trésor,
> videz-le d'un coup, vous êtes ruinés. (p.116)

In a moment of sad lucidity Mme de Beauséant finally accepts this unpalatable truth, drawing the conclusion that love is never equal, and that the partner who loves more will always be made to suffer by the one who feels less strongly. The experiences of Mme de Beauséant express an old and pessimistic concept of love, and link her with many tragic heroines including Mme de Tourvel in *Les Liaisons dangereuses* and Mathilde de la Mole in *Le Rouge et le Noir*.

The most original treatment of the theme of love in *Le Père Goriot* is the portrayal of the relationship between Delphine de Nucingen and Rastignac, a young man so different from the gentle lovers in the novels of Scott. His first ambition was to court Anastasie de Restaud, chosen for her high social status and voluptuous body, and already he imagined himself strutting through high society as her lover. It is not till the failure of this plan that he turns his attention to Delphine and makes a declaration which is entirely insincere: 'En vous voyant, quand je suis entré, je me suis senti porté vers vous comme par un courant' (p.163). The falsity of these platitudes is brutally exposed by the revelation of Rastignac's inner thoughts as he cynically thinks of Delphine as a mare which he will mount in order to progress along the road of self-advancement.

Balzac then moves away from the old theme of man as deceiver and amusingly shows the initial failure of Rastignac's schemes. In reality Delphine and Rastignac are two deceivers who finally form an alliance, and the irony of the situation is that a relationship which originated in falsity becomes sincere. The sexual factor plays an important role in the affair, and expresses Balzac's

theory that the duration of a relationship is proportional to the length
of time which elapses before consummation takes place. Rastignac is
still a virgin when he is finally admitted to Delphine's bed, and while
the young man waits for her to finish her bath on the evening when
she is going to reward his patience, the narrator intervenes with an
explanation of Parisian love. It is a unique social phenomenon, he
asserts, and demands much from the female partner:

> L'amour à Paris ne ressemble en rien aux autres amours.
> Ni les hommes ni les femmes n'y sont dupes des montres
> pavoisées de lieux communs que chacun étale par
> décence sur ses affections soi-disant désintéressées. En
> ce pays, une femme ne doit pas satisfaire seulement le
> cœur et les sens, elle sait parfaitement qu'elle a de plus
> grandes obligations à remplir envers les mille vanités
> dont se compose la vie. (p.251)

The narrator comments ominously that high-society love tends not to
last, and may bring devastation in its path. This is not quite true of
Rastignac and Delphine, who live out one of the less unsatisfactory
love-stories in Balzac's fictional world, and illustrate Balzac's theory
that love depends on equilibrium. They have similar emotional,
sensual and social needs, and take part in a fair exchange in which
each partner gives something to the other. Much of the interest of
Rastignac's situation lies in the fact that he is aware of the defects of
the woman to whom he has become addicted. His attachment to
Delphine is not some ideal and altruistic sentiment, but a self-seeking
and impure one which is part of Balzac's ironic and original study of
love.

Love in Balzac's fictional world is a complex sentiment which
is influenced not only by sentiment and social considerations, but
also by sexuality. The theme is forcefully expressed in the first pages
of *Le Père Goriot,* where the peeling varnish on the statue of Cupid
makes a symbolic allusion to venereal disease. In a statement which
is clearly out of tune with the prosaic reality of their modern urban
existence, an inscription on the base of the statue informs Mme
Vauquer's clients that their lives are ruled by Love. The residents of

the boarding-house certainly believe in the power of sexuality, being convinced for example that the young women who come to see Goriot are his paid mistresses. Vautrin confidently sees the retired merchant as a representative of a whole category of men who will ruin themselves financially to pay for their pleasures. Mlle Michonneau too knows all about such matters, as she is a former prostitute who was once attractive to men, but who has had to abdicate her power in her old age and put up with the taunts of Vautrin. We have seen that the sordid side of eroticism is also known to Delphine, who reveals to Rastignac that she had degrading experiences with Henri de Marsay (p.191). The power of Eros is again expressed in her affair with Rastignac, as she avidly seeks the satisfaction which had always been missing from her life. In his portrayal of the working of sexuality in Delphine, Balzac enters an area of human life which had been neglected by French novelists since the eighteenth century. Equally piquant in his study of other aspects of love, he shows a self-destructive tendency in Anastasie and Mme de Beauséant, since both of these women love too much, want to be deceived, and enjoy their pain.

Controversially, Balzac sees this masochistic streak as a common female instinct, and shows it also in Laure de Rastignac when she exclaims : 'Une femme doit trouver bien du plaisir à souffrir pour celui qu'elle aime!' (p.131). In his fictional world love is neither a sublime essence nor an emotional state that is constant for all individuals, but a highly variable phenomenon. It may thrive on protection, as is illustrated by Delphine and Rastignac, to whom she gives gifts and an apartment. Another example of this is provided by the affection of Vautrin for Rastignac, and the criminal has already been in prison to shield another young man loved by him. The sentiment of love is therefore often linked to that of gratitude, as is shown by both of these relationships. Balzac shows love to be dependent on individual character and circumstance, and therefore highly varied. His study of the old topos is unsentimental and rational, and in his fictional world there is little sign of the magic potion taken by Tristan and Iseut. One can describe his new version of the old theme as ironic, but it is not wholly sceptical since there is a sympathetic portrayal of Delphine, Anastasie and Mme de Beauséant in their aspiration to emotional happiness.

Marriage is one of Balzac's major themes, and *Le Père Goriot* contains no fewer than three dysfunctional couples in the Beauséants, the Restauds and the Nucingens. The theme of happy marriage is not completely absent since it is represented by the Rastignac parents and the Goriot couple, but the subject of virtue and serenity is an unpromising one for novelists, and therefore remains a minor part of the Goriot story. The subject of arranged marriages had been treated by generations of novelists, many of whom had portrayed the custom critically and asserted the importance of free choice and individual happiness instead of social and financial considerations. Balzac's portrayal of the Beauséant couple is an implicit continuation of this old theme which had already been expressed in his *Physiologie du mariage* (1828).

There is nothing essentially tragic in his account of this aristocratic marriage in which the husband tolerates his wife's love of another man. The attitude of M. de Beauséant to his wife is genteel and magnanimous, and he is portrayed as a man of worldly wisdom who has made an intelligent decision. According to Balzac, a man in the situation of M. de Beauséant could choose either vengeance or acceptance, and by his tolerance he gains peace and good relations with his wife. Balzac's sympathetic attitude to the wronged husband is expressed with wry humour in the scene where he makes a mild and gentlemanly protest when learning of his wife's decision to leave their home for ever: 'Vous avez tort, ma chère, d'aller vous enfermer à votre âge!' (p.286). The ironical twist in the story of the Beauséant couple is the fact that the wife will experience more unhappiness in extra-conjugal love than in her marriage with the tolerant Viscount. Her experience reveals an unwritten law which rules the fictional world of Balzac: in liaisons between a married woman and an unmarried man the lover will always abandon her in the end. She will then find the disenchantment of a forsaken mistress more painful than the dissatisfaction of a frustrated wife.

Delphine de Nucingen and her husband illustrate a different part of the spectrum of conjugal problems, since their bad marriage was not arranged but freely chosen. The outcome conveys the message that a union founded on social ambition is likely to lead to unhappiness, despite being wanted by both partners. Delphine and

Nucingen married each other for reasons of financial status and
formed a couple of two incompatible individuals, and the case of
Nucingen reflects Balzac's belief that a man whose life is absorbed
by a compulsive attitude to a profession will not take sufficient time
to satisfy his wife either emotionally or physically. We have noted
that Delphine's sexual frustration is expressed more than once, and
one of Goriot's first revelations to Rastignac is that she has never
known 'les douceurs de l'amour' (p.170). This hint can be placed
beside her earlier confession about 'les brutalités du mariage'
(p.162), a remark which is probably intended by the novelist as an
allusion to a traumatic sexual initiation when she was a young bride,
another theme from *Physiologie du mariage*. Balzac reveals a
situation where Delphine is aware of the power given her by her
husband's frustrated desire, and is prepared to use it. Though his
sexual preferences are repugnant to her, and possibly deviant, she is
ready to commit what amounts to an act of prostitution in order to
extract money from him: 'je saurai le manœuvrer. Il m'aime, eh bien,
je me servirai de mon empire sur lui pour l'amener à me placer
promptement quelques capitaux en propriétés' (p.261). Delphine's
calculating attitude to her power is confirmed by her statement to her
sister when she says : 'je me sentais capable de tout pour te secourir,
même d'entrer dans la chambre de mon mari' (p.267).

Added to the sexual discord between Delphine and her
husband, there is a bitter feud over money, since Nucingen has
restricted her to a fixed monthly allowance owing to her excessive
spending habits, and has illegally used her fortune in his risky
investments. As in the Beauséant marriage, the wife is the main
victim of the marital discord, but she is not the only one, and even
the insensitive Nucingen is not immune from the drawbacks of the
situation. Having coldly chosen his wife as if he were selecting an
investment, he has to live with a woman who dislikes and despises
him, but to whom he is tied by bonds of desire which can be
compared to the 'chaînes d'or' (p.177) about which Delphine
complains. One observes that the conjugal problems of Balzac's
fictional world have a symmetry which is part of his vision of the
logic of human affairs.

A variant of the theme of conjugal disharmony is provided by
the couple formed by Anastasie and her husband. Like her sister,

Anastasie is not a dutiful daughter who passively accepted an arranged marriage, since she freely chose Restaud for his social status as a member of the old aristocracy. Restaud was in love with his beautiful young wife, a fact which makes his case different from that of Nucingen, but does not save the couple from disaster. Restaud was also aware of the financial advantage represented by a marriage with Anastasie; their union is therefore based on a mixture of social calculation and personal inclination. He is a husband beyond reproach, and the ruin of their marriage will happen because of Anastasie's reckless passion for a man who exploits her financially in order to continue his obsessive gambling. Anastasie can at first control the situation, and maintain friendly relations between her lover and a husband who is blind to the danger. Her misdeeds are revealed when she secretly sells the Restaud family jewels to pay the latest debts of her lover, and her brief happiness ends in disaster. She has sacrificed her honour and her marriage to Maxime, who then coldly abandons her, and her story is a repetition of the message that an errant wife can lose both her husband and her lover. Anastasie's life is full of deceit, and hides a furtive prostitution in which she must share herself between lover and husband so that Restaud can continue to believe that he is the father of her children. The story of Anastasie could be subtitled The Dangers of Adultery, and should in itself suffice to answer those critics of Balzac who accused him of encouraging female readers to seek sexual adventures.

In *Le Père Goriot* Balzac does not draw a totally pessimistic picture of the state of matrimony. His illustrations of conjugal disharmony concern the Parisian upper class, and must not obscure the portrayal of happy marriage in the provincial Rastignac family, and in the middle-class marriage of Goriot. Balzac gives a variety of different examples of marriage, and an equal variety of opinions about the conjugal state. The attitude of Vautrin in his advice to Rastignac is purely negative and cynical: those who marry for money have to debase themselves, fawn on their mother-in-law, and are bound to be unhappy, he asserts; he adds that most marriages in Paris conceal bitter struggles about money, infidelity, or children. Balzac provides some confirmation of Vautrin's observation about Parisian marriages in the revelations from Delphine about a husband who applies financial pressure to obtain sexual favours:

> Ne serais-je pas la dernière des créatures si j'achetais son argent au prix où il veut me le vendre! Comment, moi riche de sept cent mille francs, me suis-je laissé dépouiller? par fierté, par indignation. Nous sommes si jeunes, si naïves, quand nous commençons la vie conjugale! (...) Le mariage est pour moi la plus horrible des déceptions, je ne puis vous en parler: qu'il vous suffise de savoir que je me jetterais par la fenêtre s'il fallait vivre avec Nucingen autrement qu'en ayant chacun notre appartement séparé. (p.180)

The narrator then intervenes with a sympathetic comment on the predicament of Delphine, and asserts its exemplary value as an illustration of the shortcomings of contemporary marriage customs:

> Ce mélange de bons sentiments, qui rendent les femmes si grandes, et des fautes que la constitution actuelle de la société les force à commettre, bouleversait Eugène, qui disait des paroles douces et consolantes en admirant cette belle femme, si naïvement imprudente dans son cri de douleur. (p.182)

Such themes and comments make it is easy to see why Balzac was the favourite novelist of his female readers, and Delphine's conjugal drama is conceived as a demonstration of a problem experienced by many women. The possibility of a solution is also implied by Balzac, though he is far from believing that he has a recipe for universal felicity. The figures of Delphine and Anastasie are an ingenious new version of the old complaint expressed by so many novelists since Rousseau, that marriage was too rarely based on love.

Balzac's treatment of the theme of women in society was recognised by his contemporary admirers as one of the foundations of his success, though Sainte-Beuve belittled this achievement and accused him of exploring intimate parts of female life which a gentleman would leave untouched. The role of educated female readers was crucial not just for the commercial success of a novelist, but also for the establishment of a reputation as a writer of superior quality. Nobody was more aware of this than Balzac himself, and we have noted that his preface for the 1835 edition of *Le Père Goriot* amply illustrates his sensitivity to the opinions of female readers, answering those who had written to acccuse him of including too many unfaithful wives in his novels. Some had complained that these characters were fashionable ladies who might be taken as role models by readers in spite of their fictional misfortunes. We have seen that Balzac responded by saying that he had decided to satisfy some of the discontent of virtuous female readers by limiting the introduction of more adulteresses, and had done this by his newly invented method which consisted of recycling some characters already created in earlier works, namely Mme de Beauséant, Mme de Langeais and Mme de Restaud. This left Delphine de Nucingen as the only new wife in the Goriot story. Behind Balzac's bantering tone as he gave this explanation one can detect some signs of a serious intention since he apparently did want to communicate the idea that the subject of virtue in literature is limited, whereas that of vice is varied, and inevitably more interesting. The 1835 preface promised his critics that he would soon create a highly moral heroine who would silence his censors once and for all. Time revealed her to be the virtuous Mme de Mortsauf in *Le Lys dans la vallée,* published in 1836.

No such paragon of female virtue can be found among the major figures in *Le Père Goriot,* and it is no accident that Victorine remains a minor part of the cast, since the character amply illustrates Balzac's theory about the limitations of virtuous virgins as a literary subject. Unlike many novels of the time, *Le Père Goriot* does not give a systematically flattering portrait of the female sex: Mme Vauquer is grasping and potentially cruel; with her sexual interest in Goriot and Vautrin she is portrayed as a randy and grotesque old woman. In addition, there is a suggestion that she has some malevolent, witch-like power, as her wish that Goriot should die like a dog actually comes true. There is also some mystery in her past, and a hint that it may have been disreputable. There is no doubt about the sordid antecedents of Mlle Michonneau, as we learn that she is a retired prostitute with an unconvincing story of unrewarded sacrifice, and her cold and sinister nature is represented by her skeletal appearance. Mme de l'Ambermesnil, the false Countess who swindles Mme Vauquer, is another example of treachery. However, the greatest figure of female danger is Anastasie de Restaud, who represents a peril which is all the greater because it hides behind a seductive exterior.

Apart from Mme Vauquer, who is an interesting example of an economically independent middle-class woman, Balzac's most significant female figures represent high society. He attributes to them a strong influence on social advancement, and Rastignac is rapidly propelled upwards as soon as he enjoys the protection of Mme de Beauséant. She tells her young friend about the power of the aristocratic ladies whose name will open any door, and explains that he must acquire a mistress who will be his advertisement, the confirmation of his talent, and the foundation of his future success. The rest of the action in the Goriot story is designed to show the validity of Mme de Restaud's analysis, as Rastignac will indeed achieve social advancement in his role as Delphine's lover. Balzac rarely portrays female solidarity in high society, which he represents as a milieu full of jealousy and false appearances, but his depiction of the women of this social circle is fundamentally sympathetic.

Delphine and Mme de Beauséant illustrate the problems of dissatisfied young women, and Balzac looks critically on Delphine's social ambition but favourably on her search for happiness. Young wives like herself and Anastasie are surrounded by temptation in the form of charming and dangerous young men such as Henri de Marsay and Maxime de Trailles. When they succumb, their adultery is explained by a desire for emotional experience which Balzac portrays as an essential part of the female psyche. Like the moth to the candle, the Balzacian heroine is attracted to love, even though she may burn in the flame. Often discontented, eager to live more intensely, hiding her frustration like a guilty secret, she is more sentimental than the male, and more vulnerable. She may be false and devious in pursuit of a man, like Delphine in her capture of Rastignac, but only to make sure of his affections. Inside Anastasie and Delphine there is a longing for an ideal, and also a melancholic suspicion that they may be hoping for too much. These imperfect individuals are different from noble fictional heroines made unhappy by love. The mode of their portrayal is essentially realist, despite a few lyrical notes, and their impact on the minds of Balzac's first generation of readers certainly owed much to this. In reality, Balzac replaced the traditional idealisation of women in the sentimental novel with what one can call a new dramatisation of female life. Women too have their battles to fight, says Mme de Beauséant to Rastignac, when she learns that she has been abandoned by her lover (p.119). Delphine has her share of conflict, and Balzac's account of her struggle with husband and lovers is a contribution to a new literary portrayal of what writers used to call the fair sex. Delphine is an ordinary woman who seeks personal fulfilment and makes mistakes along the road, and despite a note of authorial irony she is portrayed as a creature following a natural law. The ending of her story will be no less prosaic than the beginning, and Delphine will one day be reminded that love may not last for ever, as is recounted in *La Maison Nucingen.*

The theme of family is an important element in *Le Père Goriot*, being central and explicit in the main character, and strongly present elsewhere. The lives of Goriot, Restaud, Taillefer and Rastignac provide four significant examples of family situations, three of them with serious problems. In a direct reversal of the Goriot position, Taillefer is a cold father who rejects his daughter, and thus Balzac methodically gives his version of life's infinite variety, since the situation of virtuous Victorine is the exact opposite of that of Goriot's selfish daughters. The reason for Taillefer's rejection of Victorine is the false belief that she is the result of his wife's adultery; we see here a repetition and reinforcement of the subject which is more fully developed in the Restaud story.

A contrast is provided by the Rastignac family, which is conceived as a social model of teamwork and loyalty. Eugène's mother and sisters do not hesitate when he asks them to send their meagre savings to him, and he regards the money as a contribution to their common future. His ambition for financial success is fuelled by the need to provide the dowries without which his sisters cannot find husbands, and without which his younger brothers cannot have a good education. His gratitude is real and altruistic: 'Oh! oui, se dit Eugène, oui, la fortune à tout prix! Des trésors ne payeraient pas ce

dévouement. Je voudrais leur apporter tous les bonheurs ensemble'
(p.133). His family represents not only financial support, but a
system of moral values which are expressed in his mother's letter
urging him to remain honest. Eugène will finally abandon these
family principles, turning his back on a quiet existence as a country
gentleman living on a modest estate, but does so with regret. His
physical possession of Delphine is a turning-point in his inner
conflict between honesty and corruption, order and disorder, family
and mistress, and the outcome is clear: 'Depuis deux jours, tout était
changé dans sa vie. La femme y avait jeté ses désordres, elle avait
fait pâlir la famille, elle avait tout confisqué à son profit' (p.281).
With these metaphors Balzac confirms the symbolic significance of
the Rastignac family, which represents virtue and social stability. It is
an interesting paradox that Eugène's departure from the path of
honesty will allow the rest of his family to survive as a model of
traditional morality.

Balzac's history of the Goriot family studies its evolution over
a period of two generations, and indicates paternal error as the main
cause of disintegration. Unlike the heroines of many earlier novels,
these daughters are not the victims of paternal authority but suffer
from a lack of it, and a day comes when Delphine actually reproaches
her father for having allowed her too much freedom (p.260). The
novelist uses Goriot's dying speech to express his belief in the
importance of wise paternity, which he sees as one of the foundations
of society. In the metaphoric texture of the old man's words can be
seen the symbolic figure of Lear, the fallen King behind the fallen
merchant. Once he has realised his error, Goriot says: 'Je n'ai pas su
me conduire, j'ai fait la bêtise d'abdiquer mes droits' (p.296). Here
the thematic parallel between the Lear tragedy and Balzac's novel is
clear. The sacrifice of paternal wealth has made both men helpless in
a world where power comes from property and money, rather than
from moral principle. The realisation comes too late, as Goriot feebly
invokes the abstract rules of nature and society:

> Mes filles, mes filles, Anastasie, Delphine! je veux les
> voir. Envoyez-les chercher par la gendarmerie, de force!
> la justice est pour moi, tout est pour moi, la nature, le
> code civil. Je proteste. La patrie périra si les pères sont

foulés aux pieds. Cela est clair. La société, le monde
roulent sur la paternité, tout croule si les enfants n'aiment
pas leurs pères. (pp.295-96)

This last protest by Goriot is a dramatic expression of the theory that
society itself depends on the maintenance of the traditional family
structure.

The theme of class is an important one in *Le Père Goriot*,
which provides a systematic study of a whole social spectrum which
includes aristocrats, criminals, the police, manual workers, clerical
workers, the middle class, and the class of high finance and low
morals. It can be said that the social category represented by
Nucingen is portrayed more unfavourably than any other group,
including the criminals. Even Inspector Gondureau acknowledges the
loyalty shown by the latter, their high state of organisation, their
discipline, their intelligent choice of a leader in Vautrin whom he
describes as their Bonaparte, a man who inspires affection as well as
respect. Gondureau himself is no paragon of virtue, and is eager for a
pretext to shoot Vautrin dead, thus saving society the trouble of
giving him a fair trial. In Balzac's system of zoological comparison
he plays the role of the cunning fox, whereas Vautrin is a lion. In a
famous passage the narrator explains that the criminal is also: 'le type
de toute une nation dégénérée, d'un peuple sauvage et logique, brutal
et souple' (p.233), and in a series of strong metaphors he is described
as 'un poème infernal', and a fallen archangel.

This portrayal of Vautrin as an energetic and proud rebel
against the laws of society contrasts with that of the financier
Nucingen, to whom no good quality is given. This can be seen in the
pages where Delphine describes how her husband's methods are
based on systematic deception and fraudulent bankruptcy. Unlike
Vautrin, with his charisma and vitality, Nucingen is a low and
stealthy form of life. Balzac heaps unattractive qualities on the dodgy
financier: he is fat, sexually repulsive, untruthful, crooked, prepared
to let his wife sleep with another man, and cannot even pronounce
French properly. The accumulation of money is the main purpose of
Nucingen's life, and the role given to the unscrupulous capitalist in
the Goriot story, who continues elsewhere in Balzac's fictional

world, is sufficient to explain the interest shown by Marxist readers. According to Balzac's own untenable theory, there is no such thing as a favourable or unfavourable representation of any social group in his fiction, only a scientific objectivity. At one point, however, he uses not the voice of the narrator but that of Vautrin to make a pronouncement on social class which is certainly a reflection of the author's theoretical position: 'Je n'accuse pas les riches en faveur du peuple: l'homme est le même en haut, en bas, au milieu' (p.145).

In reality there is a gap between theory and practice, since Balzac clearly pays homage to the old aristocracy represented by the Rastignac family and by Mme de Beauséant. Even the names of these characters underline the compliment, as Beauséant contains the descriptive words 'beau' and 'séant' which highlight her superior nature, and the name Eugène comes from Greek words meaning nobleman. The whole Rastignac family, though living on a low income and struggling in the mercantile society of modern times, represents the essence of nobility in the original meaning of the word. This quality is not an accident of birth, but the personification of an ethical code. The figure of Mme de Beauséant is Balzac's homage to the privileged group which had dominated Restoration Paris, and in his comments on the elegance, wealth and taste of this class Balzac reveals his ambition to be accepted as the novelist of the aristocracy. This is the explanation of the blatant political motivation behind the narrator's assertion that the problems of Mme de Beauséant prove that: 'les personnes les plus élevées ne sont pas mises hors de la loi du cœur et ne vivent pas sans chagrins, comme quelques courtisans du peuple voudraient le lui faire croire' (p.287). It is, however, important to note that beside the noble figure of Mme de Beauséant the novelist places the cold Mme de Langeais and the unscrupulous dandy Maxime de Trailles. Despite his words of discouragement to rabble-rousers and some heavy compliments to the aristocracy, Balzac's portrayal of this class is in reality a complex and partly critical one.

The subject of money which is interwoven with the theme of social class but not identical to it, is an important part of Balzac's social analysis and one of his most obvious contributions to the thematic diversity of the French novel. In the narration of Goriot's decline in the boarding-house Balzac does not content himself with a brief and abstract statement, as other novelists of the time would have done, but gives precise details of the financial situation including the rent paid for different rooms. Monetary and personal details are inextricably interwoven in the portrait of the old man whose progressive lack of income affects the colour of his hair, the quality of his clothing, his weight and even his facial appearance. Precise economic fact is also an essential part of the portrayal of the struggling Rastignac family whose annual cash income is only 3000 francs, of which the annual sum of 1200 francs is invested in sending Eugène to Paris. Vautrin reveals to him the financial reality of the life of a fashionable young man needing fine clothes, money for gambling, and a thoroughbred horse. The total is a large one, and all is priced with precision. The narrator explains the debts of Delphine and Anastasie and the methods used by Nucingen to increase his wealth, also Goriot's financial expedients. A final example of the pervasive theme of money is seen in the episode of Goriot's death where Rastignac pawns his watch to buy medecine, after which we learn the exact cost of a cut-price funeral in 1819. Finance intervenes again in the last pathetic scene when Rastignac has to borrow twenty *sous* in order to tip the gravediggers. Though Balzac was not the first French novelist to mention money, no writer had incorporated the theme of economic reality into fiction in a manner as systematic and as forceful as this.

Le Père Goriot gives a new dimension to the old literary theme of Paris, a subject which would also inspire contemporary writers such as Eugène Sue as well as major novelists of the next generation. It is the most Parisian of Balzac's novels, starting and ending with powerful evocations of the physical presence of the city. Balzac's Paris has a double nature, being at once the city of the rich and that of the poor, and the first pages focus on the dirty gutters, crumbling plaster, the dismal streets of the old Latin Quarter where dark colleges rise up like prisons. The other Paris is a city of luxury and glitter with theatres full of light and aristocratic homes where elegant people dance beneath chandeliers. This city of the rich is a feast for the eyes, it is full of flowers and exquisite meals served on rich tables; a source of addictive pleasure; a place of encounter and of social magic which launches brilliant careers in an instant.

Life is fast and eventful in Balzac's Paris, where bad fortune too plays its role, as is seen in the lives of Goriot, Vautrin, and Mme de Beauséant. Good fortune smiles on Rastignac, the young hunter who soon fills his bag. It is Vautrin who uses the metaphor of the chase and compares the big city to a primeval forest in which success has replaced morality, since nobody cares how the hunter makes his kill:

> Celui qui revient avec sa gibecière bien garnie est salué, fêté, reçu dans la bonne société. Rendons justice à ce sol hospitalier, vous avez affaire à la ville la plus complaisante qui soit dans le monde. Si les fières aristocraties de toutes les capitales de l'Europe refusent d'admettre dans leurs rangs un millionnaire infâme, Paris lui tend les bras, court à ses fêtes, mange ses dîners et trinque avec son infamie. (p.148)

Balzac's Paris is indeed this harlot city which tolerates a delinquency that is personified not only by Vautrin and the accomplices who visit him silently in the night, but by the professional killer Franchessini and by the murderer Taillefer.

Vautrin reveals to Rastignac that Paris hides a ruthless struggle for survival in which individuals must eat each other like spiders in a pot (p.144), and the vision of the city as a place of combat is not only figurative but real. We see it when Maxime de Trailles, on meeting Rastignac, at once considers him as a rival and contemplates the possibility that he may one day kill him in a duel. Rastignac himself is ready to participate in this violent code of honour, and in a fit of anger against Anastasie he is ready to kill her lover: 'J'apprendrai (...) à tirer le pistolet, je lui tuerai son Maxime!' (p.119). In another moment of irritation the reckless young man comes near to challenging Vautrin to a duel, and there is a smell of gunpowder even in the words of Mme de Beauséant, who asks Rastignac whether he would be ready to kill for her. The theme of violent death recurs yet again when M. de Restaud reveals that he had considered either shooting Maxime in a duel or surprising him and Anastasie in bed and killing them.

The subject becomes reality when the brother of Victorine is killed in a duel which is a murder by another name. Vautrin for his part announces the imminent execution of the villain Fil-de-Soie who has betrayed him to the police. Violent death, therefore, is a familiar event in the life of Balzac's Paris, high and low. Danger lurks even beneath the glossy surface of high society, and Vautrin advises Rastignac to take shooting lessons if he wants to dance with the ladies of the aristocracy. The Balzacian city is also the scene of a conflict between the police and a criminal army which is described as a rebel nation fighting on 'le champ de bataille de la civilisation parisienne' (p.114). The pessimism of Balzac's picture of the great struggle for existence in a violent city is softened by examples of altruistic solidarity such as Rastignac's kindness to Goriot. Bianchon and Rastignac also stand together on the Parisian battlefield like the warrior friends of ancient literature, as Balzac renews the old theme of friendship among men, and adapts it to the modern urban world.

We have seen that the subject of morality was of concern to Balzac, and we have noted his response to criticism of some of his female figures on this account. There was nothing new about such attacks, and indeed the whole novel genre had often been branded as a frivolous and even subversive one which provided a fanciful and unwholesome view of reality. In his preface to *Le Père Goriot*, Balzac hit back at critics who accused him of failing to censure Goriot and Vautrin sufficiently for their immorality, and claimed that he had shown these characters to be in conflict with the laws of society. However, it is a fact that an author's interpretation of his own work may not coincide with that of his readers, and literary history provides more than one example of such ambiguity of meaning.

It is true that *Le Père Goriot* is punctuated by comment on ethical questions, but it does not amount to a clear and simple moral discourse. Even the voice of the narrator is not without ambiguity, as can be seen in the discrepancy between his opening statement and later episodes. He first tells us that his account of unfeeling Parisians is as horrible as the sight of empty skulls in the catacombs beneath the city streets (p.45), but his manner in narration betrays a fascination which is akin to respect. Far from showing disgust at the vices of humanity, the narrator sees them effectively as an intrinsic and necessary part of our nature, and explains that: 'ce que les moralistes nomment les abîmes du cœur humain sont uniquement les décevantes pensées, les involontaires mouvements de l'intérêt personnel' (p.153).

In this way Balzac avoids the platitudes of traditional moralists and adopts a less censorious attitude, as we see in the narrator's comments on Rastignac's conscience at a critical point in the action. Molière and Walter Scott had portrayed virtue and uprightness in famous literary characters, whereas Balzac would show his originality by representing the opposite in Rastignac:

> Peut-être l'œuvre opposée, la peinture des sinuosités
> dans lesquelles un homme du monde, un ambitieux fait
> rouler sa conscience, en essayant de côtoyer le mal, afin
> d'arriver à son but en gardant les apparences, ne serait-
> elle ni moins belle, ni moins dramatique. (p.165)

In his enthusiasm for the aesthetic and dramatic quality of Rastignac's progression, the narrator does not exploit his last opportunity to provide a moral discourse in the final lines of the novel when the young man makes his decision. Rastignac's alleged challenge is not the beginning of some moral campaign to make society change its wicked ways, but a decision to use them. The episode would have had less impact if the narrator had imitated orthodox moralists by preaching about the depths of the human heart, and the final scene, where Rastignac casts a cold eye on life and death, shows Balzac's creative instinct to be stronger than his didactic one.

The discourse of moral orthodoxy in the Goriot story comes most clearly from Mme de Rastignac and Bianchon, with a variable contribution from the narrator, but Balzac also introduces other powerful voices whose assertions are far from being a fictional version of the Ten Commandments. The first of these major statements comes from Mme de Beauséant, and her advice to Rastignac makes no mention of any requirement to love one's neighbour:

'Plus froidement vous calculerez, plus avant vous irez.
Frappez sans pitié, vous serez craint. N'acceptez les
hommes et les femmes que comme des chevaux de poste
que vous laisserez crever à chaque relais, vous arriverez
ainsi au faîte de vos désirs.' (p.117)

She adds that high society is cold and vicious, a moral desert where
reputation and success are everything, where the bonds of family,
love and friendship count for nothing, a world of dupes and
deceivers.

A very similar discourse on social morality is expressed by
Vautrin, and Balzac ensures that the reader will notice the parallel
between the opinion of the aristocrat and that of the criminal by
making Rastignac comment on it (p.151). Vautrin too urges him to
accept that virtue and honesty are a fatal impediment to anyone who
wants to succeed in contemporary Paris:

'Savez-vous comment on fait son chemin ici? par l'éclat
du génie ou par l'adresse de la corruption. Il faut entrer
dans cette masse d'hommes comme un boulet de canon,
ou s'y glisser comme une peste. L'honnêteté ne sert à
rien.' (p.144)

He explains that evidence of success by corrupt methods is all
around, for example in wives with an extravagant life-style supported
by prostitution, and in civil servants who get rich on bribes and buy
country estates, while the virtuous minority delude themselves that
they will receive a reward in heaven. Humanity is flawed, says
Vautrin, so there is no point in seeking perfection in oneself. Real
men see themselves as hunters in the forest and use every method at
their disposal. The superior individual understands that laws are
artificial abstractions above which he must place himself: 'Il n'y a
pas de principes, il n'y a que des événements; il n'y a pas de lois, il
n'y a que des circonstances: l'homme supérieur épouse les
événements et les circonstances pour les conduire' (p.149). The
narrator's brief and occasional words of censure on Vautrin appear
weak and conventional beside the forceful eloquence of the

criminal's long speech to Rastignac. No doubt Balzac did not create Vautrin in order to persuade young men to consider a career in crime, but the attitude of the novelist to this fictional character is intriguing. We sense that a substantial part of his analysis of contemporary Paris is indeed that of Balzac.

Another major statement on the subject of morality is woven into Goriot's final speech to Rastignac, and it is a part of his education in the lessons of life. The old man sees that his relationship with his daughters was ruined by indulgence, and he reflects that if he had not given his fortune away he would be living in a fine house with his daughters beside him. Goriot then utters his most poignant and challenging statement: 'L'argent donne tout, même des filles' (p.294). Balzac's belief in the truth of this bitter maxim is suggested by the events of Goriot's life, in which poverty destroys respect, status, and family cohesion. The situation of the Rastignac family also illustrates the power of financial reality, and Eugène learns that happiness does not buy money. In the final analysis the disenchanted and subversive maxims of Mme de Beauséant, Vautrin and Goriot seem more powerful than the voice of moral orthodoxy. In reality we have seen that Balzac speaks with a medley of voices, and the authorial viewpoint cannot be reduced to the opinions expressed by any one of them, not even the voice of the narrator. This gives the novel that element of opacity and ambiguity which is so often the mark of great literature.

Le Père Goriot is therefore a debate about moral issues, but one which does not conclude; its author is a descriptive moralist rather than a prescriptive one, an artist rather than a preacher. The Goriot story contains some comments about the possible existence of a divine Providence which might one day reward virtue and punish vice, and Vautrin speaks sarcastically of the idea, explaining that he takes it upon himself to make up for the deficiency of Providence. Rastignac for his part attempts to cling to the reassuring belief that there is a God who will eventually set things right, but cannot believe that it will happen in this world: 'Il y a un Dieu! Oh! oui! il y a un Dieu, et il nous a fait un monde meilleur, ou notre terre est un non-sens' (p.300). It is true that Balzac's fictional world does show the possibility of retribution, and Goriot himself predicts that his daughters will one day be punished by their own children. This is another expression of Balzac's theory of equilibrium, as is the fact that the thief and murderer Taillefer pays for his crimes by the loss of his son. The same principle applies to the adulterous wives like Anastasie who will one day be punished, not by Providence but by their lovers. There is no perfect justice in the lives of Goriot and his daughters, but some logic can be seen, and it makes Balzac's fictional world into something less harsh than the moral chaos feared by Rastignac.

The novelist in Balzac is never divorced from the historian, and Rastignac's moral decline is declared to be significant of a general tendency in the early nineteenth century. Balzac did not share the naïve and influential belief of thinkers such as Rousseau and his modern disciples that there ever was a golden age of virtue, but he did believe that there were fluctuations in public morality caused by the impact of historic events like the Revolution. He rejected not only the idea of a perfect state of Nature in the past, but also the notion of some future utopia, and this distances him from the optimism of Marx as it does from that of Rousseau. As Vautrin puts it, the world should be accepted as it is: 'Croyez-vous que je le blâme? du tout. Il a toujours été ainsi. Les moralistes ne le changeront jamais. L'homme est imparfait' (p.145). Not only is human nature imperfectible, but it is the same in all social classes, and the poor are no better than the rich.

Vautrin again probably speaks for Balzac when he postulates the equality of certain forms of delinquency, since the actions of Maxime de Trailles who brings adulterous children into another man's family are as criminal as those of a thief who steals the family money. We have seen that Balzac portrays Vautrin more favourably than the ruthless dandy who manipulates Anastasie and destroys a family, but he also observes Maxime without distaste, since he sees him to be acting according to his nature as a predator. As the zoologist observes the habits of a lion or a wolf without disapproval, so Balzac portrays the activities of Vautrin, Maxime and Nucingen in a manner which is essentially similar. The destruction of Goriot is a personal tragedy, but it is also a result of his own errors and a part of the nature of things, a small incident in the great struggle of Parisian life. His life-story contains comedy as well as tragedy, retribution as well as injustice, and illustrates the working of a natural system. Balzac's fundamental theme is human energy in pursuit of pleasure and survival in a naturally imperfect world. In the final analysis his protest against the modern urban jungle is a mild one.

5. Epilogue

Rastignac, Vautrin, Nucingen, Delphine, Anastasie, and Mme de Beauséant continue their pursuit of fortune, power or happiness in other works by Balzac. *La Femme abandonnée*, which was already published before *Le Père Goriot* was written, is an account of the experiences of Mme de Beauséant when she has left the glittering world of high society. After her emotional disappointment in the capital she goes to hide her sorrow in a country cottage, where she lives in solitary contemplation of her error in loving a man she could not marry. She then makes exactly the same mistake again by falling in love with a young man called Gaston de Nueil. With him she enjoys three years of happiness, after which he bows to family pressure and agrees to end the affair and marry a suitable person. The sublime but incorrigible Mme de Beauséant is wounded again in her struggle against the nature of things. She is crushed by the rules of society, and a victim of her own emotions.

The future career of Vautrin, on the other hand, is a story of success which is narrated partly in *Illusions perdues*, where he forms with the desperate young Lucien de Rubempré the criminal pact rejected by the more prudent Rastignac. His adventures continue in *Splendeurs et misères des courtisanes* where he tricks Nucingen out of a large sum of money, but is caught. Vautrin finally changes sides in the war between criminals and society, and is recruited by the police. *La Maison Nucingen* narrates the future career of the banker, who continues his dubious financial operations with great success, and whose social rise will be complete when he is elevated to the peerage after the Revolution of 1830. The career of Rastignac is equally brilliant, thanks to his association with Nucingen, who accepts the young man as his wife's lover, and uses him as a business accomplice. Rastignac's early experiences in Mme Vauquer's house have hardened him and eradicated his youthful scruples, and he finally achieves wealth and high social status as a cabinet minister. His love-affair with Delphine, on the other hand, leads to disenchantment and a bizarre ending. His youthful passion gives way to boredom and gradual indifference, as he becomes tired of his role as escort to a lady of fashion, obliged to share her life of frivolity, her moods and her caprices. They do remain lovers for fourteen years, after which he slowly disengages himself, and they separate amicably. Delphine then feels the real sting when her husband offers Rastignac the hand of her daughter Augusta. He represses whatever scruples he may have about marrying the daughter of his former mistress, accepts the offer, and is set to inherit the Nucingen fortune. Nucingen has now rewarded his faithful associate, and amused himself by an act of vengeance on his errant wife. In this cruel episode Balzac completes a satirical portrayal of high society morals which would be much admired by Proust (*28*).

It is not surprising that such themes and characters aroused debate among the professional critics of Balzac's time, who wanted to inform potential buyers of the moral tendency of novels which might get into the eager hands of their adolescent daughters. The appeal of *Le Père Goriot* in particular was rapid and considerable, its dramatic quality and impact on the popular imagination being attested by the appearance of two competing stage adaptations shortly after publication of the novel. This sort of theatrical version was the nineteenth-century equivalent of films inspired by successful novels in modern times, with the difference that the authors received no payment, though they could benefit from the publicity and hope for increased sales.

Far from disapproving of stage adaptations on principle, Balzac himself actually considered producing his own dramatic version of the Goriot story. The quality of the work was so evident that scrupulous critics could not dismiss it as a shocking tale by a talented but immoral novelist. Writing in the prestigious *Revue de Paris* in 1835, the young critic Guéroult paid homage to him as the leading French novelist and praised the creator of Delphine for the psychological truth and finesse of his female figures. Guéroult sought to explain much of Balzac's success by his achievement in this fictional area:

> M. de Balzac est l'historien privilégié des femmes, il
> excelle à traduire les causes secrètes et inaperçues de

leurs déterminations, à rendre les traits les plus délicats
de leur mobile physionomie; mais ce n'est pas encore là
que le dernier de ses titres auprès d'elles; il s'est presque
partout constitué leur avocat, leur protecteur; il a su faire
valoir avec un art infini toutes les douleurs rentrées dont
elles suffoquent à l'insu de tous, il a répandu du charme
et de l'intérêt jusque sur le délaissement des vieilles
filles. M. de Balzac est le conteur par excellence,
l'homme des nuances et des détails; il ne se contente pas
d'indiquer une situation, il la termine, il l'achève, il vous
dira avec précision les conséquences que doivent amener
dans une même situation morale les différences de
fortune et de position; c'est le peintre d'intérieur, et
comme de juste, le favori du public féminin. (*9*, p.189)

By the time of the publication of *Le Père Goriot* the name of Balzac
was well known throughout Europe. In Britain there was a
considerable market for his novels, which were imported in their
original versions and eagerly read by a public attracted by their
thematic audacity, which made them so different from novels of the
home production. Many professional reviewers of new fiction,
however, felt obliged to warn readers of the grave moral danger
which they saw lurking in these foreign works.

In April 1836 a long and unsigned article in the conservative
Quarterly Review contained a violent denunciation of Balzac in
general and of the Goriot story in particular: '*Le Père Goriot* (...) is
the longest, and as we understand the most admired of M. de
Balzac's *Scènes de la vie*. Strange must be the life of which it can be
a representation!' (*10*, p.91). In the world of Balzac, complains the
reviewer, all the main females are adulteresses, and Rastignac is a
sordid modern usurper of the role once held by the noble-minded and
attractive young aristocrats who were formerly the protagonists of
French novels. And this unsavoury portrayal of the aristocracy is
flanked by an even less appealing picture of the middle class, laments
the London critic, who declares his aversion to the description of a
boarding-house which is 'a den of filth, penury, envy and malignity'.
The critic concludes his evaluation of the novel with a final piece of

dismissive sarcasm: 'If M. Balzac's French admirers – who must be so much better judges – had not assured us that this was 'an admirable picture of *real* Parisian life', we should have pronounced it a clumsy tissue of odious exaggerations.' Despite such denunciations, or because of them, the reputation of *Le Père Goriot* as Balzac's finest work continued to grow throughout Europe.

As late as 1852, however, there were still virulent attacks on the work from established critics, including one by Charles de Mazade in the *Revue des deux mondes*:

> Un des caractères tristement irrécusables du talent de M. de Balzac, c'est que, au milieu de facultés diverses et vigoureuses, il manquait complètement d'un certain idéal élevé, d'une certaine règle supérieure capable de diriger, de contenir et de féconder son observation, de donner à ses qualités tout leur prix. Moralement, il en est résulté que l'auteur des *Scènes de la vie parisienne* franchissait le plus souvent toutes les bornes, confondait tous les éléments, et ne savait nullement discerner la limite au-delà de laquelle les passions, les sentiments, les caractères cessent d'être vrais humainement pour devenir des exceptions difformes et repoussantes, qui ont tout au plus leur place dans quelque musée Dupuytren de la nature morale. Il est arrivé plus d'une fois au roman moderne de rivaliser avec ce *panthéon* élevé à toutes les turpitudes physiques. Je ne citerai qu'un exemple dans les œuvres de M. de Balzac, c'est *Le Père Goriot*. Est-ce là encore de la réalité? Je l'ignore. (*13*, p.235)

It is reassuring to observe, on the other hand, that Balzac's singular talent was recognised by such creative writers as George Sand, Stendhal, Hugo, Gautier and Baudelaire.

Flaubert, whose only reservation concerned Balzac's style, made an eloquent homage to him in *L'Education sentimentale*. One indication of this can be seen in the episode where Frédéric Moreau is introduced to the banker Dambreuse, and Deslauriers urges the young protagonist to imitate Rastignac by becoming the lover of the financier's wife. Later events confirm that Flaubert's novel is an adaptation of the Rastignac story, a new and ironic version in which the incompetent Frédéric does become the lover of the banker's wife, but fails to achieve even a career based on corruption. Flaubert's great story of Parisian life is the most lasting compliment ever paid to Balzac. Just as the author of *Le Père Goriot* had taken themes and situations from *King Lear,* so Flaubert had drawn inspiration from him. The power of Balzac's theme is further confirmed by its reappearance in *Crime and Punishment* by Dostoievski, where the situation of Raskolnikoff contains clear allusions to that of Rastignac.

Henry James was another major novelist of the nineteenth century who admired the author of the Goriot story, describing him as one of the finest artists as well as one of the coarsest. Although he spoke of what he called Balzac's incomparable power, James claimed that he overloaded his fiction by including too many facts of history, finance, and sociology. The American novelist also continued the narrow and censorious tradition of Anglo-Saxon puritanism when he accused Balzac of having no natural sense of morality. He did not go so far as to repeat Thackeray's remarkable assertion that Balzac, for this reason, was inferior to his obscure but uncontroversial contemporary Charles de Bernard.

These dismissive comments tell us much about Balzac's originality, and his powerful effect on readers throughout Europe. However, it is true that there is no such thing as bad publicity as far as novels are concerned, and warnings about decadence only served to make many readers more eager to explore the morally dangerous world of Balzac. One of the most surprising opinions about Balzac was expressed by James when he claimed that the author was at his best when he portrayed simple virtue. If this were really true, characters like Bianchon would have had greater impact in the Goriot story and elsewhere, and we have seen that Balzac himself was convinced of the difficulty of making a virtuous character interesting. James places his finger on an essential characteristic when he complains that the author of *Le Père Goriot* usually evaluates conduct with a judgment which is not moral but aesthetic.

The essay on Balzac by Henry James was soon followed by a homage from Zola, who claimed him as a predecessor in *Les Romanciers naturalistes (15).* The articles by James and Zola are particularly interesting because they came from major novelists, and indicate his influence on the genre itself. This has continued throughout the twentieth century, and Proust himself drew inspiration from them. The controversy aroused by Balzac's fictional world focuses on three aspects which can be called aesthetic, moral and political. Aesthetic criticism has usually concerned itself with matters such as style and alleged exaggeration. Flaubert had never accused his predecessor of the latter, being convinced that all great creators of fictional characters consciously used overstatement. He saw it as a respectable and even fundamental literary mode which was exploited by Molière in his time. We can agree that figures such as Vautrin owe some of their impact to a literary process of enlargement, and also to the inclusion of a symbolic dimension. For the greater part, however, the Goriot story is a portrayal of ordinary individuals in a physically detailed contemporary setting, and is therefore the essence of that modern realist fiction to which Balzac contributed so much. As for criticism of *Le Père Goriot* on aesthetic grounds, one should not apply inappropriate Flaubertian criteria to a very different writer, but instead give him credit for his very real virtues. Balzac was not a slow and disciplined worker like Flaubert, but had his own natural qualities of spontaneity, originality, imagination and power.

We have seen that the debate on the moral tendency of Balzac's fiction began at the time of publication of his novels, and it is a remarkable fact that talented writers like Janin, Sainte-Beuve and even Thackeray were among his detractors. The passing of time has enabled us to see their negative reaction as a part of what can be called the Balzac phenomenon. The nature of his themes was such that controversy was bound to be aroused, just as his success aroused envy among other writers. In our own century the debate has been more measured. Is thed world-view of Balzac essentially Christian, as argued by Guyon, or Marxist, as claimed by a series of admirers from Lukács to Barbéris? Is Freudian theory, as seen in the study by Marthe Robert, the key to the meaning of his works?

The fact that Balzac's fictional world has inspired so many critical approaches is confirmation of its significance and depth. The interest of Marxist readers in *Le Père Goriot* is easy to understand, such is the role given to the theme of class and to economic factors, and the figure of Nucingen can indeed be seen as an attack on unscrupulous capitalism, though Balzac does not either predict or advocate the rise of the proletariat. A Freudian reading of the Goriot story may focus on the theory of wish fulfilment in the creation of Rastignac, or on the theme of the delinquant mother who brings adulterous children into her family, since this was a situation which Balzac had experienced in his own life. The prudent reader may wish to note, without dwelling on them, such possible thematic transfers from life to fiction. To deny their existence and their interest would be artificial, but they are not the prime concern of the student of literature. We do not wish to place the author himself on the couch lest we drift too far into the unverifiable theories of psychoanalysis, and downgrade the literary work to the status of a symptom.

What is the significance of the theories and principles which Balzac either invented by himself or borrowed from contemporary thinkers? The pseudo-scientific notions of Gall and Lavater concerning the human personality make a minor contribution to *Le Père Goriot*, where they are discernable for brief moments. Gall had convinced many of his contemporaries that his system, called phrenology, could explain individual character by the shape of a person's head, and Balzac adopted this belief, as he did the similar theories of Lavater. Whatever the fragility of these ideas in the eyes of science, they form a coherent part of his fictional world, which has its own laws. He enthusiastically adopted one of the more sensible ideas made fashionable by the famous charlatan Mesmer, Vautrin's psychological power and ability to fascinate being a fictional expression of this theory. We have seen that his most important belief concerns the existence of a parallel between the animal and the human world. This is a theory which expresses itself not only in the figurative texture of the style, but in his vision of the city as a forest in which a great struggle for survival is taking place.

We have seen that Balzac believed in the historical function of the novel, and this principle is effectively put into practice in the portrayal of figures such as Goriot, Rastignac, and Nucingen. These characters personify social changes which Balzac believed to be significant in the France of his time. The truth of his assertions about the historical accuracy of his fictional creations can never be verified, but it is a fact that many of his first readers did believe that the

portrayal of Parisian society in *Le Père Goriot* contained much that
was true. This may have been caused by the persuasive power of
good writing. Art can seem more real than reality. 'Lire, c'est créer à
deux,' wrote Balzac in the eleventh meditation in *Physiologie du
mariage*, showing a very modern conception of the role of the reader.
He believed that female readers in particular tended to engage in this
creative process, responding to the attractive young male characters
in sentimental novels by bringing them into their emotional life and
giving them the status of imaginary lovers. He took care that the
Goriot story contained no such idealised young hero, or sentimental
portrayal of the human condition. On the contrary, it proclaims that
humanity is very far from perfect, and that the meek shall definitely
not inherit the earth, unless Vautrin intervenes like a satanic
Providence. It is at the same time a tragedy, a comedy, and an early
example of the modern genre which would come to be known as
crime fiction. It shows Balzac at the summit of his creative power,
bursting the framework of the traditional novel and inventing the first
broad fictional universe in which characters recur in successive
books. This was a venture in which he would be imitated by other
ambitious writers, notably Zola.

   Le Père Goriot combines literary techniques some of which
were inspired by the novels of Scott, while others were drawn from
the theatre. Balzac forged these different elements into a new and
distinctive narrative form. His account of the career of Rastignac,
starting in this novel and concluded elsewhere, is a continuation of
the recently established *Bildungsroman* genre. This ironic story of an
unheroic modern Theseus with his smart suit and gold watch is also a
new and potent version of the epic, an ancient and still venerated
literary form which had reached a terminal state of decay. The figure
of Rastignac, as an ambitious and energetic young man, would prove
to be one of the first of a series of similar characters found in the
novels of Balzac's successors, such as Zola and Maupassant. They
too saw the upwardly mobile individual as a social characteristic of
the period.

   Balzac's gift was the ability to entertain his readers while also
disturbing them with a dark vision of modern society. The lives of
Rastignac and Delphine take place in an era of rapid change which
does not seem essentially distant from us, and in their psychological

profile too the characters have an evident modernity. This is also true of the narrative form in which their fictional lives are framed, since it seems to have left an indelible stamp on French literature. Robbe-Grillet famously complained (*31*, p.15) that modern French literature was still dominated by one type of novel, based on the model created by Balzac. There is no more eloquent confirmation of his lasting achievement than this oblique homage, which was made in an article written more than a century after his death.

Select Bibliography

WORKS BY BALZAC

1. *La Comédie humaine* (Paris, Gallimard, Bibliothèque de la Pléiade, 1976-81). Edited by Pierre-Georges Castex. Volume I contains the *Avant-propos*, and Volume III an edition of *Le Père Goriot* with an introduction and notes by Rose Fortassier.
2. *Correspondance* (Paris, Garnier Frères, vol.II, 1962).
3. *Lettres à Madame Hanska* (Paris, Editions du Delta, vol.I, 1967).

STUDIES OF LE PÈRE GORIOT

4. Barbéris, Pierre, *Le Père Goriot de Balzac: écriture, structures, significations* (Paris, Larousse, Coll. Thèmes et Textes, 1972).
5. Bellos, David, *Balzac: Old Goriot* (Cambridge University Press, Landmarks of World Literature series, 1987).
6. Guichardet, Jeannine, *Le Père Goriot d'Honoré de Balzac* (Paris, Gallimard, Coll. Foliothèque, 1993).
7. Kanes, Martin, *Père Goriot: Anatomy of a Troubled World* (New York, Twayne, Twayne's Masterwork Studies, 1993).
8. Lock, Peter, *Balzac: Le Père Goriot* (London, Edward Arnold, Studies in French Literature series, 1967).

EARLY EVALUATIONS OF BALZAC *(in chronological order)*

9. Guéroult, Adolphe, 'Lettre à un ami de province sur quelques livres nouveaux' in *La Revue de Paris*, 15 août 1835.
10. Unsigned article in the *Quarterly Review*, April 1836.
11. Thackeray, William, 'On some French fashionable novels' in *The Paris Sketch Book* (London, John Macrone, 1840).
12. Sainte-Beuve, 'Dix ans après en littérature' in *La Revue des Deux Mondes*, 1 mars 1840. Article incorporated in *Les Grands Ecrivains français par Sainte-Beuve* (Paris, Garnier Frères, 1927).
13. Mazade, Charles de, 'Monsieur de Balzac' in *La Revue des Deux Mondes*, 20 août 1852.

14. Baudelaire, Charles, 'Théophile Gautier' in *L'Artiste*, 13 mars 1859. This article, partly on Balzac, is in *L'Art romantique*: Baudelaire, *Œuvres complètes* (Paris, Gallimard, Bibliothèque de la Pléiade, 1961).
15. James, Henry, 'Honoré de Balzac', in *French Poets and Novelists* (London, Macmillan, 1878).
16. Zola, Emile, *Les Romanciers naturalistes* (Paris, Charpentier, 1891).

LATER STUDIES

17. Bardèche, Maurice, *Balzac romancier* (Paris, Plon, 1947).
18. Beizer, Janet, *Family Plots: Balzac's narrative generations* (New Haven, Yale University Press, 1986).
19. Bolster, Richard, *Stendhal, Balzac et le féminisme romantique* (Paris, Lettres Modernes, Bibliothèque de littérature et d'histoire, 1970).
20. Brooks, Peter, *The Melodramatic Imagination: Balzac, Henry James, melodrama and the mode of excess* (New Haven, Yale University Press, 1976).
21. Brunetière, Ferdinand, *Honoré de Balzac* (Paris, Nelson, 1913).
22. Donnard, Hervé, *Les Réalités économiques et sociales dans La Comédie humaine* (Paris, Armand Colin, 1961).
23. Guyon, Bernard, *La Création littéraire chez Balzac* (Paris, Armand Colin, 1969).
24. Hemmings, F.W.J., *Balzac: an interpretation of La Comédie humaine* (New York, Random House, 1971).
25. Hunt, Herbert, *Balzac's Comédie humaine* (London, The Athlone Press, 1959).
26. Kanes, Martin, *Balzac's Comedy of Words* (Princeton University Press, 1975).
27. Michel, Arlette, *Le Mariage chez Honoré de Balzac: amour et féminisme* (Paris, Les Belles Lettres, 1978).
28. Prendergast, Christopher, *Balzac, Fiction and Melodrama* (London, Edward Arnold, 1978).
29. Proust, Marcel, *Contre Sainte-Beuve* (Paris, Gallimard, 1954).
30. Pugh, Anthony, *Balzac's Recurring Characters* (London, Duckworth, 1979).
31. Robbe-Grillet, Alain, *Pour un nouveau roman* (Paris, Editions de Minuit, 1963).
32. Robert, Marthe, *Roman des origines et origine du roman* (Paris, Grasset, 1972).
33. Rogers, Samuel, *Balzac and the Novel* (Madison, University of Winsconsin Press, 1953).
34. Tilby, Michael (ed.), *Balzac* (London, Longman, Modern Literatures in Perspective series, 1995).

ARTICLES

L'Année balzacienne *is abbreviated as* AB :

35. Adamson, Donald, '*Le Père Goriot* devant la critique anglaise', *AB*, 1986, pp.261-80.

36. Billot, Nicolas, '*Le Père Goriot* devant la critique en 1835', *AB*, 1987, pp.101-30.

37. Hoffmann, Léon-François, 'Les métaphores animales dans *Le Père Goriot*', *AB*, 1963, pp.91-106.

38. Lichtlé, Michel, 'La vie posthume du *Père Goriot* en France', *AB*, 1987, pp.131-66.

39. Mozet, Nicole, 'La description de la Maison-Vauquer', *AB*, 1972, pp.97-130.

40. Uffenbeck, Lorin, 'Balzac a-t-il connu Goriot?', *AB*, 1970, pp.175-82.